CHILDREN'S ENCYCLOPEDIA
OCEAN

CHILDREN'S ENCYCLOPEDIA
OCEAN

Miles
KeLLy

First published in 2013 by Miles Kelly Publishing Ltd
Harding's Barn, Bardfield End Green, Thaxted, Essex, CM6 3PX, UK

2 4 6 8 10 9 7 5 3 1

Publishing Director Belinda Gallagher

Creative Director Jo Cowan

Cover Designer Simon Lee

Designers Jo Cowan, Rob Hale, Joe Jones, Venita Kidwai,
Simon Lee, Andrea Slane, Elaine Wilkinson

Editors Carly Blake, Rosie McGuire,
Sarah Parkin, Claire Philip

Indexers Indexing Specialists (UK) Ltd,
Marie Lorimer

Image Manager Liberty Newton

Production Manager Elizabeth Collins

Reprographics Stephan Davis, Jennifer Hunt, Thom Allaway

Contributors Camilla de la Bedoyere, Fiona Macdonald,
David Parham, Steve Parker

ISBN 978-1-78209-108-0

Printed in China

British Library Cataloguing-in-Publication Data
A catalogue record for this book is available from the British Library

Made with paper from a sustainable forest

www.mileskelly.net
info@mileskelly.net

www.factsforprojects.com

CONTENTS

SEASHORE 8–49

CORAL REEF 50–91

DEEP OCEAN 92–133

WHALES AND DOLPHINS 134–175

SHIPWRECKS

SEASHORE

1 Seashores can be found all over the world, from icy coastlines near the Poles to sandy beaches in hot, tropical areas. As well as making unique habitats (natural homes) for many plants and animals, seashores are also very important to people. Today, large areas of Earth's 700,000-plus kilometres of seashores are in danger and in need of our protection.

▼ Tall columns of rock (stacks), tidal pools, seaweeds and starfish are typical of rocky shores. This peaceful summer scene is at Second Beach near La Push, Washington State, USA.

Land meets sea

2 Seashores are places where the salty water of seas and oceans meets land made of rocks, mud, sand or other material. A seashore is the edge of the land and the edge of the sea.

Wave-shaped icebergs, Iceland

ARCTIC OCEAN

Tourist centre, Mexico

PACIFIC OCEAN

NORTH AMERICA

ATLANTIC OCEAN

3 There are names for different kinds of seashores. If the rocks are tall and upright, they are known as cliffs. If the sand is smooth and slopes gently, it is a beach. Seashores are known as oceanic coasts, or marine or sea coastlines.

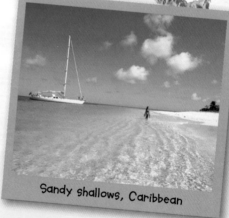
Sandy shallows, Caribbean

SOUTH AMERICA

4 Water moves easily with waves, tides and currents, so seashores are never still. They are complicated habitats for nature, as only certain kinds of animals and plants can live there. Wildlife must be able to survive in the changing conditions that are typical of most seashores.

Breaking glaciers, Antarctica

SOUTHERN OCEAN

Seafront houses, Denmark

ASIA

EUROPE

PACIFIC OCEAN

AFRICA

Tropical palm beach, Seychelles

Great Barrier Reef, Australia

OCEANIA

INDIAN OCEAN

5 In total, there are more than 700,000 kilometres of seashore. Canada is the country with the longest total seashore, at more than 202,000 kilometres. Indonesia is next, with 55,000 kilometres of seashore.

6 Some seashores are not part of the world's main network of seas and oceans. They are the seashores around the edges of large bodies of salty water that are isolated inland, such as the Caspian Sea and the Dead Sea.

ANTARCTICA

Endless battles

7 Seashores are like battlegrounds, with a continuing struggle between land and sea. The outcome depends on factors such as the land's hardness, and the strength of the winds and waves.

▶ Winds provide the energy to whip up waves that erode the shore.

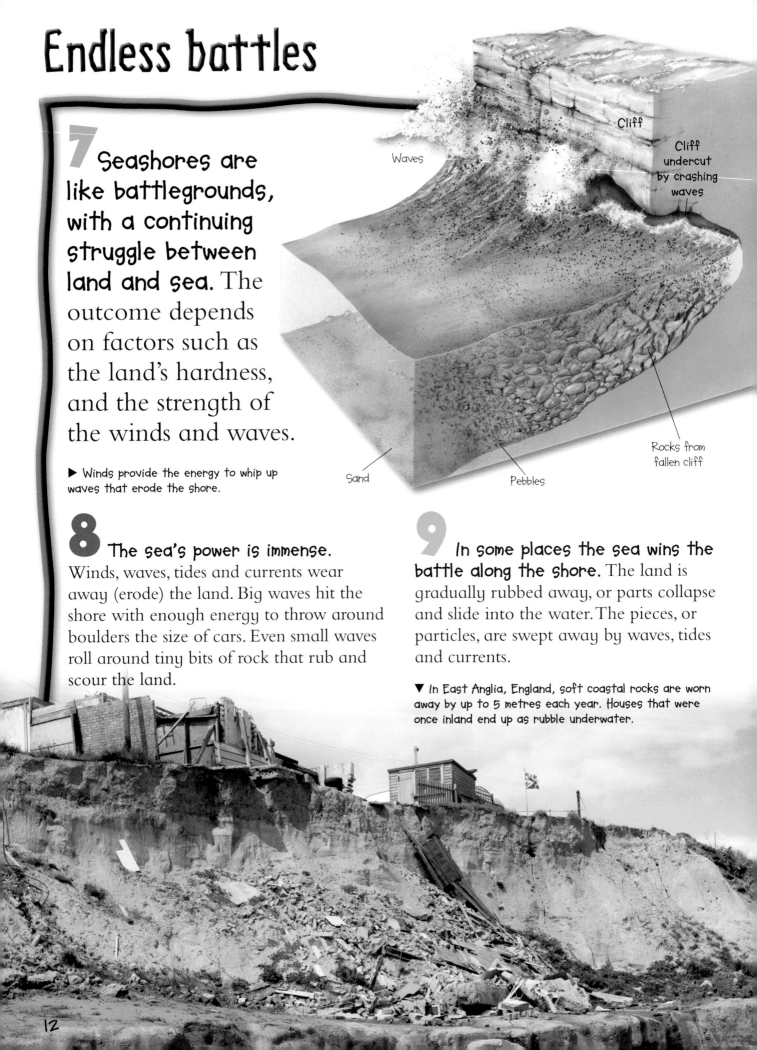

Cliff

Cliff undercut by crashing waves

Waves

Rocks from fallen cliff

Sand

Pebbles

8 The sea's power is immense. Winds, waves, tides and currents wear away (erode) the land. Big waves hit the shore with enough energy to throw around boulders the size of cars. Even small waves roll around tiny bits of rock that rub and scour the land.

9 In some places the sea wins the battle along the shore. The land is gradually rubbed away, or parts collapse and slide into the water. The pieces, or particles, are swept away by waves, tides and currents.

▼ In East Anglia, England, soft coastal rocks are worn away by up to 5 metres each year. Houses that were once inland end up as rubble underwater.

▲ These granite rocks in Nova Scotia, Canada, have hardly changed for hundreds of years.

▲ Chalk cliffs in southern England are eaten away by waves, leaving piles of broken rock at their bases.

10 How the seashore's land resists the eroding power of the sea depends on the types of rocks. Hard rocks, such as granite, are tough and can resist erosion for centuries. Softer rocks, such as chalk and mudstone, erode several metres each year.

11 In other places, the land wins the battle. New land can be formed from piles of particles, such as sand or silt, moved by the water from coasts elsewhere or from the deep sea. Particles sink and settle as layers, called sediments, that build up.

12 Movements in the Earth can change seashores. Land can bend and buckle over centuries, so coasts slowly rise. Earthquakes can lift land by several metres in a few seconds. A volcano near the coast can spill its red-hot lava into the sea, where it cools as hard, new rock.

▶ Lava meets the sea in Hawaii. Sea water makes volcanic lava cool suddenly in a cloud of steam.

CLIFF COLLAPSE!

You will need:

large, deep tray or bowl
wet play sand   water

Make a steep cliff in the tray or bowl by piling up wetted sand on one side. Then gently pour in the water. Swish the water with your hand to make waves. Watch how they eat into the cliff and make it fall down.

Tides, currents and winds

13 Almost all seashores have tides, which affect the way the land is worn away. Tides alter the amount of time that a particular patch of the shore is underwater or exposed to the air, so they also affect coastal habitats and wildlife.

I DON'T BELIEVE IT!

The tidal range is the difference in height between high and low tide. In the Bay of Fundy in Canada it is 17 metres, and in parts of the Mediterranean Sea it is less than 0.3 metres.

14 Tides are caused by the pulling power or gravity of the Moon and Sun, and the daily spinning of the Earth. A high tide occurs about 12.5 hours after the previous high tide, with low tides midway between.

Moon

Spinning Earth

Tidal bulge

◄ The Moon's gravity pulls the sea into 'bulges' on the near and opposite sides, where it is high tide. Inbetween is low tide. As the Earth spins daily, the 'bulge' travels around the planet.

15 Spring tides are extra-high — the water level rises more than normal. They happen when the Moon and Sun are in line with the Earth, adding their gravities together every 14 days (two weeks). Neap tides are extra-low, when the Sun and Moon are at right angles, so their pulling strengths partly cancel each other out. A neap tide occurs seven days after a spring tide.

▼ At new Moon and full Moon, the Sun, Moon and Earth are in a straight line, causing spring tides. At the first and last quarters of the Moon, the Sun and Moon are not aligned, so neap tides occur.

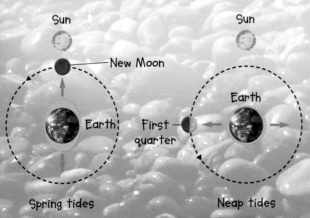

Sun

New Moon

Earth

First quarter

Spring tides

Sun

Earth

Neap tides

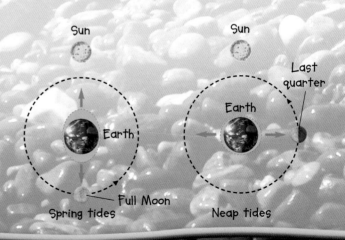

Sun

Earth

Full Moon

Spring tides

Sun

Last quarter

Earth

Neap tides

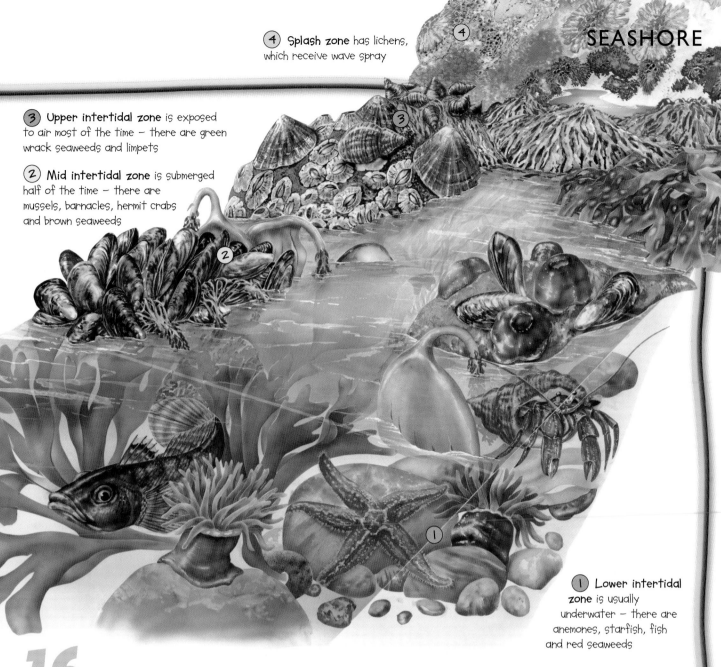

④ Splash zone has lichens, which receive wave spray

④

③ Upper intertidal zone is exposed to air most of the time – there are green wrack seaweeds and limpets

② Mid intertidal zone is submerged half of the time – there are mussels, barnacles, hermit crabs and brown seaweeds

③

②

①

① Lower intertidal zone is usually underwater – there are anemones, starfish, fish and red seaweeds

16 Tides produce 'zones' along seashores, from the high tide zone to the low tide zone. Different seaweeds and animals are adapted to each zone.

▲ The amount of time underwater determines which animals and plants live along a rocky shore.

17 Ocean currents affect the seashore. A current flowing towards the shore can bring particles of sediment to add to the land. A current flowing away sweeps sediment out to sea. Currents also alter the direction and power of waves.

18 If a wind blows waves at an angle onto a beach, each wave carries particles of sand upwards and sideways. When they recede, the particles roll back. Particles gradually zigzag along the shore – a process called longshore drift. Groynes built into the sea help to control it, so beaches don't wash away.

Seashore features

19 On a typical seashore, the struggle between land and sea produces various features. Much depends on the balance between the sea's wearing away of the land, and the formation of new land by particles settling in layers, known as sedimentation.

Stump

Needle

Stack

Arch

Headlar

20 Hard or tough rocks can resist the sea's eroding power. They form tall cliffs and headlands that erode slowly. Softer rocks break apart more easily. The waves erode them at sea level, which is known as undercutting. The whole shore collapses as boulders tumble into the water.

Shingle spit

Shingle or pebble beach

21 Waves and other shore-eroding forces may gradually cut through a headland, forming a cave. This can get worn through to form an arch of rock. When the arch collapses it leaves an isolated tall piece of rock, called a stack.

Groyne

▲ In this bay, waves and currents wash sediments with increasing power from right to left. Wall-like groynes or breakwaters lessen longshore drift.

QUIZ
Match these record-breaking coastal features to their countries.
1. The longest spit, 100 kilometres.
2. The tallest sea stack, 550 metres.
3. The tallest seashore cliffs, 1560 metres.
A. Australia B. Greenland
C. Lithuania and Russia

Answers:
1C 2A 3B

Circular bay

Cave

Cliffs

Waves

22 Waves and onshore currents flowing towards the land bring sediments to make low shores and mounds of sand, mud and silt. These can lengthen to form long spits. During extra-high spring tides these sediments grow higher.

23 Depending on winds and currents, a huge rounded scoop may be carved along the seashore to form a bay. In sheltered parts of the bay, particles of sand gather to form a beach. As the bay gets more curved, it can break through the land behind to leave an island.

River →

Delta

Mudflats (bare mud near delta)

Saltmarsh (with plants)

Sandy beach

24 The area where a river flows into the sea is a type of shore known as an estuary, or river mouth. Particles of sand and mud may build up in sheltered areas, forming low mudflats and saltmarshes.

Coast to coast

25 **A seashore's features and wildlife depend on its location.** Seashores near the Poles are cold most of the year and the sea may freeze for months. Almost no life can survive there.

◀ Antarctic coasts are mostly floating sheets and lumps of ice. Crabeater seals rest at the ice edge after feeding in the almost freezing water.

26 **Some cold seashores have no land.** Glaciers and ice shelves spread outwards, so the sea meets ice, not land. The edge of the ice may have smooth slopes and platforms cut by the waves. Jagged chunks of ice crack off and fall into the water as floating icebergs.

27 **In tropical regions around the middle of the Earth, seashore conditions are very different.** It is warm for most of the year and many forms of life flourish, including seaweeds, fish, crabs, prawns, starfish and corals.

▼ Tropical seashores include coral reefs, like this one near Komodo Island, Southeast Asia, with huge biodiversity (range of living things).

28 Exposure to wind is a powerful factor in the shaping of a shoreline. A windward seashore is exposed to strong prevailing winds. The winds make waves that hit the shore hard, sending salty spray to great heights. This type of shore has very different animals and plants from a leeward seashore, which is sheltered from the main winds.

29 Yearly seasons have an effect on seashores and their wildlife. Usually there is rough weather in winter, with winds and storms that increase land erosion. Some wildlife moves away from the shore in winter – birds fly inland while lobsters and fish move into deeper water.

30 The slope of the sea bed at the shore is very important, affecting the size and number of waves. A sea bed with a very shallow slope tends to produce smaller waves. A steep slope up to the beach gives bigger waves that erode the land faster, but are good for surfing!

LET'S SURF!

You will need:
sink or bathtub   water   tray

Put 10 centimetres of water into the sink or bathtub. Hold the tray at one end, at an angle so that part of it slopes into the water like a beach. Swish your other hand in the water to make waves hit the 'beach'. How does altering the tray's angle from low to high affect the waves?

▲ A big winter storm, such as this one in Sussex, UK, can smash even the strongest sea defences, which have to be repaired regularly.

Saltmarshes and mudflats

Sea thrift (sea pink) likes drier areas of marsh

Common cordgrass helps bind loose mud

Glasswort has fleshy leaves that store water

Sea aster flowers in late summer

▲ Saltmarsh plants have to endure harsh conditions, as they are exposed to both salt water and freshwater.

31 On a sheltered seashore, small particles of sediment collect. This happens around the mouths of rivers (estuaries). As the river's water speed slows, its floating particles sink to the bottom.

32 Saltmarshes have partly dry areas. They are rarely fully submerged, perhaps only with salty water at spring tides, or with freshwater if a nearby river floods.

▶ Many wading birds feed by probing into mud for small worms and shellfish.

Redshank

Curlew

33 Saltmarsh plants include glasswort, sea purslane, sea aster, sea lavender, sea thrift and red fescue. These plants are food for small creatures such as worms and insects, which are eaten by birds such as rails, curlews, herons and egrets.

Soft-shell clams
like muddy shores
best

Laver spireshells
are also called
mudsnails

Towershells
feed in both
sand and silt

Common cockles
filter sea water
for food

▲ Shelled animals with two shell halves are called bivalves. Spiral ones are types of sea-snails.

34 Mudflats are usually lower and wetter than saltmarshes, as every high tide washes over them. Plants find it difficult to take root in these conditions, but a few, such as rice grass, cordgrass and eel grass, manage. Cordgrass grows in the wetter regions of saltmarshes around the world. It has glands to get rid of unwanted salt taken in from sea water.

35 Most mudflat animal life is under the surface. There are burrowing animals such as ragworms, mud shrimps and ghost crabs, and shelled creatures such as spireshells, towershells, cockles and various types of clams. Birds, especially waders such as godwits, knots and snipes, fly in at low tide to probe for these creatures.

▼ Each year, summer plants grow into the calm waters of saltmarshes, spreading their greenery into the channels. However autumn storms soon wash them away.

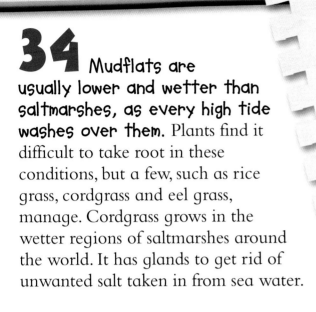

I DON'T BELIEVE IT!
In some mudflats, the numbers of small shellfish, called spireshells, are greater than 50,000 in just one square metre!

Sandy beaches

36 Sandy shores need gentle winds, waves and currents that are still strong enough to wash away silt and mud. Just above high tide, any rain quickly drains away between the grains of sand, so it is too dry for land plants to grow. Below this, the grains move with wind, waves and tides, so few sea plants can grow there either.

I DON'T BELIEVE IT!

Searching along the beach strandline is known as beachcombing. It is especially rewarding after a big storm!

37 Most sandy shore life is under the surface. Animals hide under the sand while the tide is out. As it rises, it brings with it tiny plants and animals, known as plankton, and bits of dead plants and creatures. Shrimps, lugworms, clams, tellins, scallops and heart urchins burrow through the sand or filter the water to feed.

38 Small sandy shore animals are meals for bigger predators that follow the tide, including cuttlefish, octopus and fish such as sea bass and flatfish. The giant sea bass of North Pacific shores grows to more than 2 metres long and weighs 250 kilograms.

▼ As the tide comes in, creatures hidden in the sand come out and start to feed – but predators are ready to eat them.

Jellyfish
may get washed up onto the beach and stranded

Cuttlefish
grab prey with their tentacles

Sand eels
feed on the bottom

Flatfish
have colours similar to the sea bed

Common shrimps
half-hide in burrows

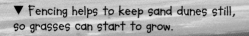

▼ Fencing helps to keep sand dunes still, so grasses can start to grow.

39
As high tide retreats, it leaves a ribbon of washed-up debris along a beach, called the **strandline.** Animals including gulls, foxes, otters and lizards scavenge here for food, such as dead fish and crabs.

40
On some sandy shores, onshore winds blow the sand grains up the beach towards the land. Mounds, ridges and hills form seashore habitats called sand dunes. Marram grass can survive the wind and dryness, and its roots stop the grains blowing away, stabilizing the dunes.

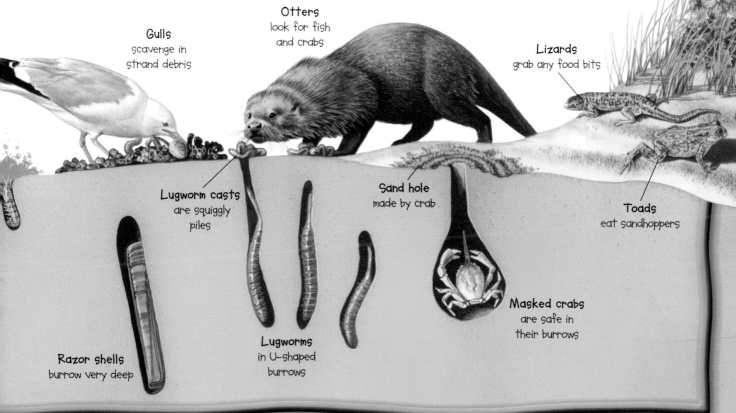

Gulls scavenge in strand debris

Otters look for fish and crabs

Lizards grab any food bits

Lugworm casts are squiggly piles

Sand hole made by crab

Toads eat sandhoppers

Razor shells burrow very deep

Lugworms in U-shaped burrows

Masked crabs are safe in their burrows

Mangrove swamps

41 **Mangrove swamps are unusual shore habitats.** They occur in the tropics where wind, waves and currents are weak, allowing mud to collect. The mud has no tiny air pockets, which land plants need to take oxygen from.

◀ Shoreline mangroves, here in East Africa, form a thick tangle where no other plants grow. These mangrove trees have stilt roots.

42 **Mangrove trees use their unusual roots to get oxygen from the air.** Some have stilt or prop roots, which hold the tree above the mud and water so it can take in oxygen through tiny holes in its bark. Others have aerial roots covered with tiny holes that poke above the mud into the air.

▼ Black mangroves, like these in Florida, USA, have aerial roots covered with tiny holes that poke above the mud into the air.

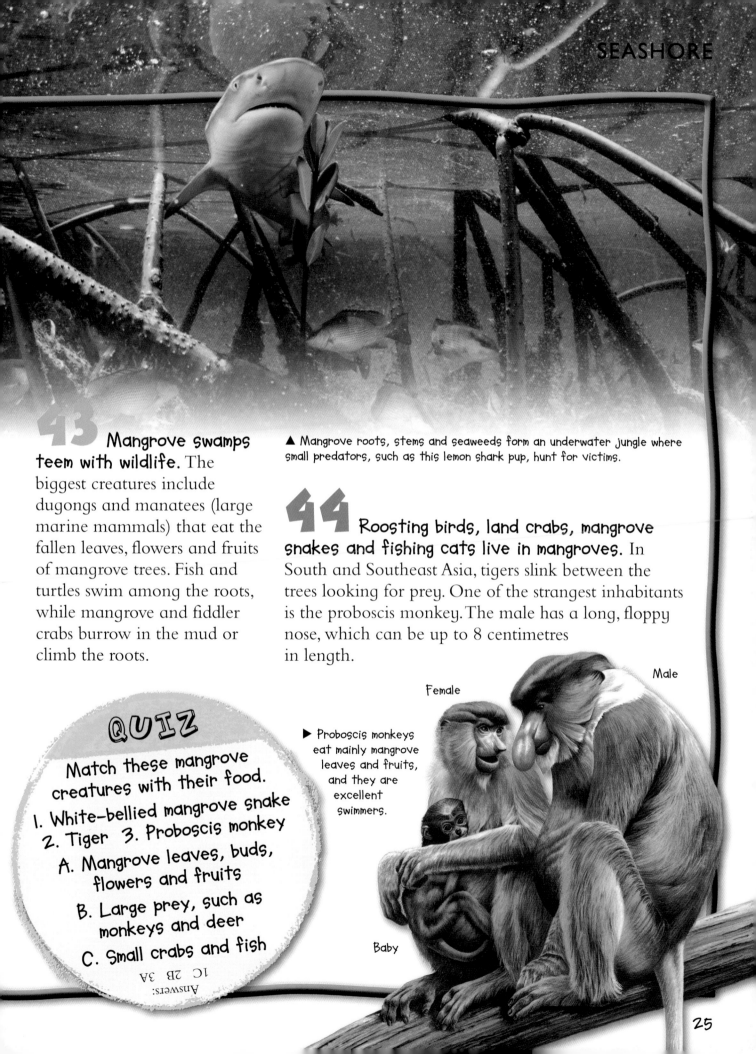

43 **Mangrove swamps teem with wildlife.** The biggest creatures include dugongs and manatees (large marine mammals) that eat the fallen leaves, flowers and fruits of mangrove trees. Fish and turtles swim among the roots, while mangrove and fiddler crabs burrow in the mud or climb the roots.

▲ Mangrove roots, stems and seaweeds form an underwater jungle where small predators, such as this lemon shark pup, hunt for victims.

44 **Roosting birds, land crabs, mangrove snakes and fishing cats live in mangroves.** In South and Southeast Asia, tigers slink between the trees looking for prey. One of the strangest inhabitants is the proboscis monkey. The male has a long, floppy nose, which can be up to 8 centimetres in length.

Female

Male

▶ Proboscis monkeys eat mainly mangrove leaves and fruits, and they are excellent swimmers.

Baby

QUIZ

Match these mangrove creatures with their food.

1. White-bellied mangrove snake
2. Tiger 3. Proboscis monkey

A. Mangrove leaves, buds, flowers and fruits

B. Large prey, such as monkeys and deer

C. Small crabs and fish

Answers:
1C 2B 3A

25

Shingle and pebbles

45 One of the harshest seashore habitats is the shingle, pebble or gravel beach. Fairly strong winds, waves and currents wash away smaller particles, such as silt and sand, leaving behind lumps of rock and stone. Sand or mud may collect over time, but a strong storm's crashing waves wash them away.

◀ On this New Zealand shingle beach, a storm has washed away some of the smaller pebbles to leave a line of larger cobbles, which protect the shingle higher up the beach.

HIDDEN EGGS

You will need:

smooth, rounded pebbles tray
watercolour paints and brush
three hen's eggs

Lay out the pebbles on the tray and look at their colours and patterns. Paint the hen's eggs to match the pebbles. Place the eggs among the pebbles. Are they so well camouflaged that your friends can't spot them?

46 Waves roll shingle and pebbles around, wearing away their sharp edges and making them smooth and rounded. Plants are in danger of being crushed by the waves, but oysterplant, sea kale and sea blite gain a roothold. Lichens, combinations of fungi or moulds, and simple plants known as algae, coat the stones.

◀ Sea kale usually grows just above the high tide mark.

Ring-like black band around neck

Camouflaged eggs

Fleshy folded leaves

Plentiful small white flowers

47 Animals forage along the strandline, where debris is left by the receding high tide. Ringed plovers, little terns and oystercatchers lay their eggs in a small scrape or hollow. The eggs are perfectly camouflaged because they look similar to the pebbles around them.

▲ The ringed plover checks its eggs before going off to feed on small creatures.

48 Shingle and pebble shores are very mobile. Storms and powerful currents can shift them from place to place, or even wash them into the sea. Pebbles can build up over years into a long ridge called a shingle spit. The spit shelters the sea behind it and allows other kinds of coastlines to form, such as mudflats, lagoons or sandy beaches.

◀ The 16-kilometre shingle spit of Orford Ness, east England, is bare on the seaward side, but has plants on the sheltered side bordering the River Alde.

Estuaries and lagoons

▲ This maze of channels and sandbanks at the mouth of Australia's Murray River changes over months and years, especially during winter storms.

49 **An estuary is the end of a river at the coast, where it flows into the sea.** The river might emerge through a narrow gap. Or it can gradually widen as it approaches the sea, so that at the shore it is so wide you cannot see from one side to the other.

50 **The river water slows down as it flows into the sea and loses its movement energy.** As this happens, its sediment particles settle out in order of size. This is known as sediment sorting or grading. As particles settle to the bottom, they may form a spreading area in the river mouth called a delta.

51 **Estuaries are halfway habitats, with freshwater towards the river and salt water towards the sea.** There is an ever-changing mixture inbetween due to tides, currents and rainfall. This partly salty water is known as brackish.

▶ Grizzly bears dig up tasty shellfish on an estuary beach in Canada.

▶ This circular island in the Maldives, called a coral atoll, has a lagoon in the middle.

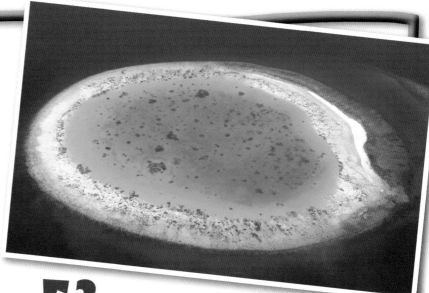

52 A lagoon is a sheltered area behind some kind of barrier, such as a ridge of shingle or a coral reef. Protected from the full force of the waves, lagoons are usually calm, warm, shallow and full of life.

▼ Blacktip reef sharks often gather in shallow lagoons and estuaries in the breeding season to find partners and mate. They lay eggs here, where the baby sharks are safer from large predators than in the open water.

53 The tallest inhabitants in some coastal lagoons are flamingos, such as the American and greater flamingo. They filter tiny shrimps, shellfish and plants from the water with the brush-like bristles inside their beaks.

29

Rocky shores and pools

54 Where the land is made from hard rock, different kinds of rocky shores form. They vary with the rock's hardness, the size of the pieces, and whether the shore is exposed to wind, waves and currents. Tidal zones are usually visible on these shores with 'lines' of seaweeds.

▲ Some seaweeds, such as kelps, have a sucker-like part, the holdfast, to fix them to rocks.

55 Channelled wrack, a green seaweed, often grows high on the shore with bladderwrack. Knotted rack grows slightly lower. Towards the low tide area are brown seaweeds, such as oarweeds and kelps, and even lower are red seaweeds. These plants vary depending on the coast's exposure to wind and waves.

▼ Seaweeds anchor to any stable object, such as these mostly buried rocks on a beach in France.

KEY

1. Anemone
2. Mussel
3. Goby
4. Bladderwrack seaweed
5. Hermit crab
6. Topshell
7. Limpet
8. Razor shell
9. Sea urchin
10. Sponge
11. Shore crab
12. Velvet crab
13. Prawn
14. Starfish

▼ A busy rock pool is a mini-habitat crawling with plants, herbivorous animals and predators.

56 Fixed-down creatures such as barnacles and mussels live on the bare rocks of the mid-tidal zones. As the tide comes in they filter tiny edible particles from the water. Limpets hold onto the rocks firmly and move slowly, scraping off plant growth. Seaweeds form forests for smaller animals such as shellfish, crabs, prawns, and fish such as gobies and blennies, as well as starfish, anemones, sea mats and sea squirts.

57 Seashore rock pools are left behind as the tide retreats. They are miniature communities of animals and plants. The seaweeds capture the Sun's light energy for growth. Herbivorous animals such as periwinkles and limpets eat the plants. Predators ranging from whelks to octopus hide among the crevices and prey on the herbivores.

Visitors to the shore

58 **Many animals visit seashores.**
Some of them come to feed or breed.
Others stop there to rest during long
journeys or to escape danger such as
predators or harsh conditions inland or
out at sea. Otters like to catch fish and
crabs in the pools and shallows.

▲ Sea lion pups may feed on their
mother's milk for up to one year.

◀ Male Southern elephant
seals roar and fight rivals
on the beach. Winners get
to mate with females.

59 **Seals, sea lions and walruses
are ideally suited to diving, swimming
and feeding at sea.** But they come ashore
to beaches or rocks to rest and sunbathe.

60 **Seals and sea lions have
their young (pups) along the
seashore.** The pups feed on their
mothers' milk, then stay ashore while the
mothers return to the sea to catch food.
Within two or three weeks the pups can
swim and dive.

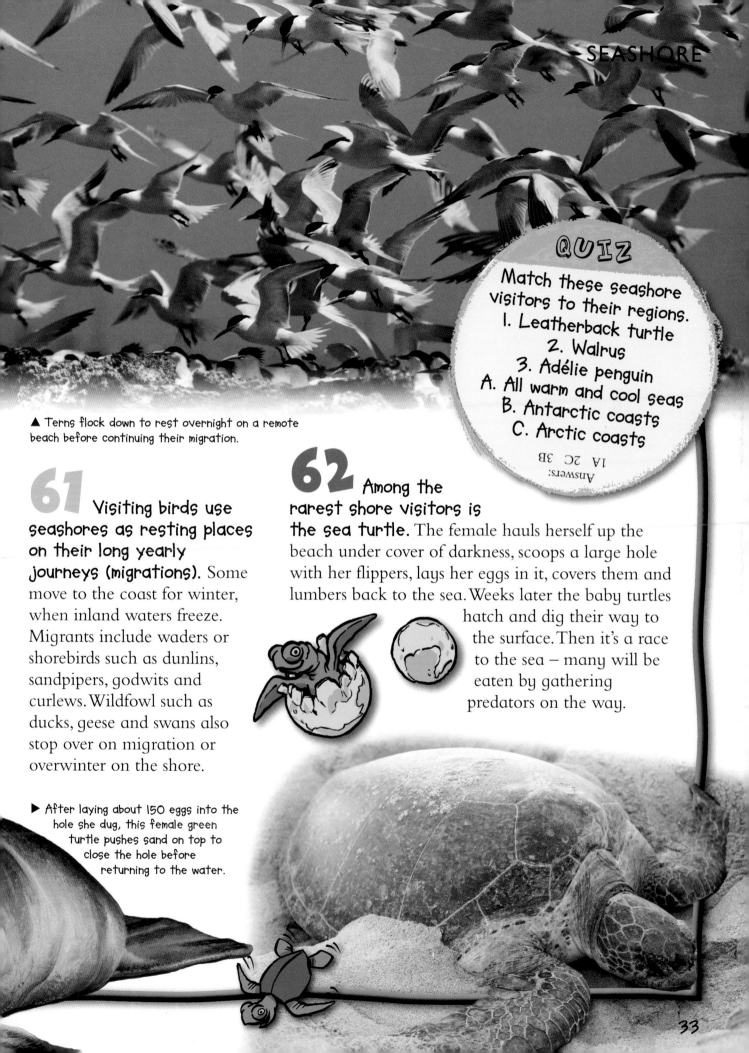

▲ Terns flock down to rest overnight on a remote beach before continuing their migration.

QUIZ

Match these seashore visitors to their regions.
1. Leatherback turtle
2. Walrus
3. Adélie penguin
A. All warm and cool seas
B. Antarctic coasts
C. Arctic coasts

Answers:
1A 2C 3B

61 Visiting birds use seashores as resting places on their long yearly journeys (migrations). Some move to the coast for winter, when inland waters freeze. Migrants include waders or shorebirds such as dunlins, sandpipers, godwits and curlews. Wildfowl such as ducks, geese and swans also stop over on migration or overwinter on the shore.

▶ After laying about 150 eggs into the hole she dug, this female green turtle pushes sand on top to close the hole before returning to the water.

62 Among the rarest shore visitors is the sea turtle. The female hauls herself up the beach under cover of darkness, scoops a large hole with her flippers, lays her eggs in it, covers them and lumbers back to the sea. Weeks later the baby turtles hatch and dig their way to the surface. Then it's a race to the sea – many will be eaten by gathering predators on the way.

33

Above the seashore

63 The skies above many seashores are busy with all kinds of flying animals. Several kinds of birds rest or nest along the shore, flying out to sea or inland to feed.

◀ Different kinds of birds tend to perch and nest at different heights along the cliffs.

64 Coastal cliffs are safe nesting places for many different seabirds. It is difficult for predators, such as foxes, lizards or snakes, to reach the birds' eggs and chicks on steep rocky ledges. Cliff-nesters include fulmars, puffins, Manx shearwaters and gannets.

KEY

1. Great black-backed gull
2. Lesser black-backed gull
3. Herring gull
4. Rock dove
5. Chough
6. Puffin
7. Guillemot
8. Razorbill
9. Rock pipit
10. Fulmar
11. Kittiwake
12. Black guillemot

65 **As darkness falls along the shore, most birds settle to rest.** The nocturnal (night-time) fliers such as owls and bats come out. The coastal sheath-tail bat of Australia and Papua New Guinea feeds mainly on beetles and other insects. Along the shores of southwest North America, the fishing bat swoops down to catch fish, crabs and other creatures.

▲ The caracara, a type of falcon, pecks the flesh from mussels.

66 **Some birds fly along coasts when looking for food, including gulls, waders, wildfowl and birds of prey.** There are several types of sea eagle, including the bald eagle (national emblem of the USA) and the even more powerful Steller's sea eagle.

67 **Flying insects are also common along seashores, especially in the summer.** Beetles and flies buzz around washed-up rotting seaweeds, fish and other debris. Butterflies flutter along the upper shore and cliffs, searching for sweet nectar in the flowers. They include the bitterbush blue butterfly of Australia, and North America's rare Lange's metalmark butterfly, which inhabits sand dunes.

▶ Grayling butterflies sunbathe on sea holly and shore rocks.

Sea holly

I DON'T BELIEVE IT!

The peregrine falcon hunts along the shore as well as inland. It kills other birds by power-diving onto them at speeds of more than 200 kilometres an hour, making it the world's fastest animal.

Skins, shells and stars

68 Many kinds of small seashore fish, such as gobies, shannies and blennies, don't have scales. They are covered in tough, smooth, slippery skin. This helps them to wriggle through seaweed and slip away from rolling pebbles.

▲ The soft-bodied hermit crab uses an empty sea-snail shell for protection, finding a larger one as it grows.

▼ Mudskippers can stay out of water for several hours and 'skip' on their front fins.

69 Crabs scuttle and swim across the shore. They have eight walking legs and two strong pincers (chelae). Many are scavengers, eating whatever they can find. Others hunt small fish and similar creatures. Their long-bodied cousins are lobsters, which grow to one metre long.

FISHY FACTS!

You will need:
notebook   pen

Next time you're in a supermarket or fishmonger, look for the various kinds of fish and shellfish on sale – cod, salmon, prawns, mussels and so on. Make a list of them. Do some research and find out which ones live along seashores – probably quite a few!

70 Seashore anemones look like jelly blobs when the tide is out and colourful flowers when it's in. Anemones are predatory animals. Their stinging tentacles grab fish, shrimps and other prey, paralyze them, and pass them to the mouth.

71 Starfish are slow but deadly hunters. They grab shellfish such as mussels, and gradually pull their shell halves apart. The starfish then turns its stomach inside out through its mouth, and pushes this through the gap between the shell halves to digest the flesh within.

▼ The scallop snaps its two shell valves shut, creating a jet of water that pushes it away from danger, such as a hungry starfish.

72 Shellfish abound on the seashore. Whelks and topshells have snail-like curly shells. Cowries have beautifully patterned shells in bright colours. Bivalve shellfish such as clams, oysters, cockles and scallops have two halves (valves) to the shell.

▶ Goose barnacles are related to crabs. Their feathery feeding tentacles filter tiny bits of food from sea water.

Seashore dangers

73 Seashores can be hit by many types of natural disasters. Among the most deadly are giant waves called tsunamis. These are usually set off by underwater earthquakes, volcanoes or landslides, which shake the sea bed and push water into massive ripples that spread out until they reach a shore.

③ Wave gets taller but slower as it approaches the coast

② An upward wave is formed

④ Wave crashes or breaks onto the coast

① Undersea earthquake moves large amount of water

▲ As tsunami waves enter shallow water, they move more slowly but grow taller.

74 The high winds of hurricanes, typhoons and tornadoes can whip up giant waves. They crash on the shore, smash buildings, flood far inland and cause immense destruction. In 2008, typhoon Nargis hit Burma (Myanmar) in Southeast Asia. It killed more than 200,000 people, made millions homeless, and flooded vast areas with salt water, making the land useless for growing crops.

▼ Tsunamis can flood whole towns along the coast, washing salt water and mud everywhere. Houses were flattened near the coast of Banda Aceh, Indonesia, after a tsunami in 2004.

▲ In the past being a lighthouse-keeper was a vital but lonely job, with weeks alone tending the lamp and its machinery. Today most lighthouses, such as Fanad Head in north-west Ireland, are electric and mostly automatic.

75 For centuries fire beacons, lanterns, lighthouses and lightships have warned boats and ships about dangerous shores. Hazards include running aground on a sandbank or hitting rocks just under the surface. Each lighthouse flashes at a different time interval so sailors can identify it.

Top 5 dangers to divers

1 Getting snagged or caught in old nets, cables, ropes and fishing lines.

2 Being pushed onto sharp-edged corals, underwater girders or boat wrecks by currents.

3 Waves stirring up the sea bed, making it easy to get lost in the cloudy water.

4 Poisonous animals such as sea-wasps, box jellyfish, stingrays, lionfish and stonefish.

5 Big fierce fish such as barracudas, tiger sharks, great whites and bull sharks.

▼ The stonefish's fin spines can jab deadly venom into the skin.

Venom canal

Sharp tip

Venom gland

▼ Fire coral is named after the burning pain it causes if touched.

76 Even just walking along a shore or paddling in shallow water can be dangerous, especially in tropical regions. There may be poisonous animals such as jellyfish, weeverfish, stonefish and shellfish known as coneshells, all of which have stings that can kill.

People and seashores

77 People have lived along seashores and coastlines for thousands of years. Settlers could hunt and gather food from the sea. They could travel by boat along the coast, up rivers to inland areas and across the sea to other regions. These boats carried raw materials, food and goods for trading.

78 Foods from the seashore include fish, octopus, crabs and lobsters caught with nets, spears or hooks and lines. Shellfish such as cockles, mussels, scallops, limpets and winkles are gathered by hand. Seaweeds can be harvested for food or to obtain chemicals used in many processes from dyeing textiles to glass-making.

I DON'T BELIEVE IT!

Seashore plants were once used to make glass. Glassworts, samphires and saltworts were harvested and burned to obtain the substance soda-ash, or sodium carbonate, used in glass-making.

79 Seashores are important in traditional arts, crafts and religions. Driftwood is carved into fantastic shapes, seashells are collected for their beauty, and necklaces made of sharks' teeth supposedly give strength to the wearer. Gods and spirits from the sea feature in many religions, faiths and customs, such as Kauhuhu the shark god of Hawaii.

▼ Sri Lankan fishermen perch on poles and watch for fish passing below as the tide changes.

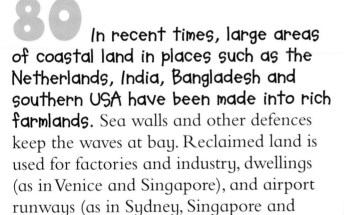

▲ Lights never go out in Hong Kong harbour, one of the world's busiest seaports.

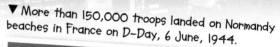

▼ More than 150,000 troops landed on Normandy beaches in France on D-Day, 6 June, 1944.

80 In recent times, large areas of coastal land in places such as the Netherlands, India, Bangladesh and southern USA have been made into rich farmlands. Sea walls and other defences keep the waves at bay. Reclaimed land is used for factories and industry, dwellings (as in Venice and Singapore), and airport runways (as in Sydney, Singapore and Hong Kong).

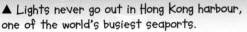

▼ Holiday developments completely destroy natural coasts, with increased travel by air and sea as tourists come and go.

81 Seashores have featured in empires and battles through the ages. Seafaring and trading centres, such as Constantinople (now Istanbul), Venice and London, were once hubs of great empires. Castles and forts keep out seaborne invaders. World War II's D-Day seaborne invasion of France's Normandy coastline in 1944 was the largest military event in history.

Seaside adventures

82 In modern times, seashores have become places for fun, leisure and adventure. People relax, sunbathe, play games and sports, and view buildings and monuments. In many countries, more than half of all tourism business is along coasts.

▲ Scuba-divers should 'take nothing but photographs and memories', leaving wildlife completely untouched.

▼ Adding just the right amount of water makes the sand firm for sculpting.

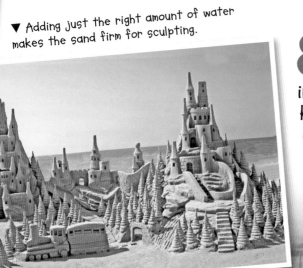

83 Fun activities at the seashore include swimming, snorkelling, scuba-diving, kite-flying and building sandcastles. People also paint, draw and photograph beautiful scenes of the waves, shore, sky and Sun. Many seaside resorts have sand sculpture competitions, where contestants produce amazing shapes from just sand and water.

84

Some seashores attract sportspeople, especially large flat beaches, which can be used by horse riders, runners and racers. Sand racing takes many forms, from land-yachts with wheels blown along by sails, to record-breaking racing cars. Softer sand is best for volleyball, football, bowls and similar ball games.

SAND SCULPTING

You will need:
half a bucket of clean play sand
large tray   small cup   water

Start with dry sand. Pour it onto the tray and try to shape it into a tower or castle. Put it back in the bucket, mix in one cup of water and try again. Then add another cup, try again, and so on. At what stage is the sand best for shaping and sculpting?

85

In shallow water along the shore, people do sports such as surfing, windsurfing, kitesurfing, waterskiing, jetskiing and paragliding. There is also rod fishing, spear fishing, beach netting and other pastimes which could result in a tasty meal.

86

Sea walls and pleasure piers extend from the shore, allowing people to stroll along, do some sea fishing or see a show in the theatre at the end. The longest pleasure pier in the world is Southend Pier in Essex, England, at 2160 metres.

▼ Bondi Beach near Sydney, Australia, is famous for its surfing and lifesaving displays – but it also gets very crowded.

▼ Pleasure piers, such as Southend Pier, were popular in the last century, but few new ones are built.

Trade and power

▶ Modern ports, such as this one in Singapore, are busy day and night all through the year.

Cities, ports and industrial centres have been set up along shores all over the world. There are harbours, docks, wharves and warehouses where cargo ships and passengers come and go, as part of global trade and travel.

88 Today's world uses energy at an increasing rate and many energy sources come through or from seashores. Petroleum (oil) and gas supertankers arrive at coastal storage centres, depots and refineries, where they load or unload their cargoes.

89 Many electricity-generating power stations are along seashores. Big ships can unload supplies of coal, oil, gas and other energy sources directly to them. Another reason is that they can use sea water to cool their generating equipment, to make electricity more efficiently.

▲ At Mossel Bay, South Africa, dozens of giant tanks store natural gas from wells out at sea.

90 Electricity can be generated at seashores, especially from the moving water of tides and waves. The flowing water turns underwater turbine blades connected to generators when the tide comes in and goes out. Wave power is more difficult to harness because big storms can smash the generating equipment.

91 Factories making products are often sited along the coast. Cargo ships bring raw materials, such as coal, oil and metal ores, and take away a wide range of finished products such as trucks. Sadly, factory wastes and unwanted chemicals may be released into the sea.

▲ The Limpet is one type of small wave-power generator being tested in Scotland.

Seashores in trouble

92 Seashores and their animals and plants face all sorts of threats and dangers. Pollution occurs in many forms, such as oil spills, chemical waste from factories, and dirty water and sewage from towns and cities. All kinds of rubbish litters the shore.

▲ In Namibia, Africa, desert comes right to the sea. Many ships have run aground and been wrecked, rusting away along this 'Skeleton Coast'.

I DON'T BELIEVE IT!

Along some busy beaches, more than one in ten particles or grains is not sand – it is plastic. Known as 'beach confetti', this plastic sand is a growing problem worldwide.

93 Seashore tourist centres and holiday resorts may be fun, but they cause big problems. They bring coastal roads, seaports and airports, bright lights, activity and noise to the shore and shallow waters. This frightens away shore creatures such as fish, crabs, seals, sea turtles and birds.

▼ This pile of plastic and other debris in Dorset, England, is typical of the pollution washed up after a storm.

94 Modern shore fishing and food harvesting does immense damage. Powerful boats with huge nets scour and scrape up life from the water and sea bed, leaving them empty. People fish with dynamite and poisonous chemicals. Unique habitats are destroyed and will take years to recover.

▲ Plastic nets and lines do not rot away naturally. They may trap animals, such as this green turtle, for months.

95 Global warming and climate change are looming problems for the whole Earth – especially seashores. Sea levels will rise, altering the shapes of coasts, wiping out natural shore habitats and man-made ones, and flooding low-lying land beyond, from wild areas to cities and rich farmland.

96 With global warming and climate change, more extreme weather may come along coasts. Hurricanes, typhoons and other storms could happen more often, causing destruction along the shores. Today's coastal flood defences, such as sea walls and estuary barriers, will be overwhelmed.

▼ Recycled materials can be used as sea walls to protect against rising sea levels – but they only last a few years.

SOS — Save our seashores

97 **Seashores need our protection and conservation in many ways.** Each shore is a unique habitat, and once gone, it may never return. With problems such as pollution coming from both the land and the sea, seashores are stuck in the middle and need extra care.

▼ Whales sometimes get stranded on beaches, perhaps because they are ill from pollution. Efforts to save them do not always succeed.

98 **One way to conserve seashores is to make them protected nature reserves, wildlife parks or heritage sites.** The area might be protected land that extends to the sea or a marine park that extends to the land. The world's biggest such park, at 360,000 square kilometres, is the Pacific's Papahānaumokuākea Marine National Monument. It includes the northwestern Hawaiian islands and the seas around.

99 You can help to protect seashores by supporting wildlife and conservation organizations, from huge international charities to smaller local ones. In the UK, contact your county-based Wildlife Trust and ask about seashore projects that might need help.

▲ Scientists travel to remote beaches to study wildlife, such as these walruses, and to find out how their seashore habitats are changing.

100 You can even help seashores on your own!

⌒ Don't drop litter or leave rubbish along the shore, and ask others not to either.

⌒ Encourage people to look after their seashores.

⌒ Join an organized beach litter-pick or shore clean-up.

⌒ Don't buy souvenirs that might have come from living wildlife, such as dried seahorses and starfish.

⌒ Tell someone in authority (police, lifeguard, coastguard) if you come across an injured or stranded animal — but do not touch it.

CORAL REEF

Beautiful coral reefs lie beneath the sparkling surfaces of sapphire-blue seas. Although they only take up a tiny amount of space in the world's oceans, coral reefs contain more than one-quarter of all types of sea creatures and are home to billions of animals and plants. Coral reefs are among the Earth's most precious places but they are in grave danger of disappearing forever.

◀ Reefs teem with life as fish dart and dash around stone-like coral structures. Panda butterflyfish inhabit reefs in tropical oceans and can grow up to 20 centimetres in length.

What are coral reefs?

102 Coral reefs are ocean habitats (homes) made by the creatures that live inside them. Tiny coral animals called polyps live together in huge numbers, known as colonies. They can grow for thousands of years, building reefs that can measure more than 2000 kilometres long.

▲ The coral reefs in the Florida Keys National Marine Sanctuary are so vast they can be seen from space.

103 Reefs are home to many animals and plants. Together, the reef and all the things living in it make up an ecosystem. Coral reefs are some of the most varied ecosystems in the world, and are thriving, colourful places that burst with life.

◄ Sea anemones attach themselves to the reef structure and fish hide away in the many nooks and crannies.

CORAL REEF KEY
1. White-spotted rose anemone
2. Club-tipped anemone
3. Gopher rockfish

104

It is not only coral polyps that help a reef to grow. Polyps provide the framework of a reef, but other living things add to the structure. Some marine (sea) organisms, such as sponges and sea cucumbers, have a hard substance called silicon in their skeletons. When they die, their skeletons add to the coral reef.

105

Land-living animals and plants also depend on reefs. In shallow water, plants take root in the mud and sand that collects around a reef. Mangrove trees and sea grasses grow here – the spaces around their roots make good places for animals, such as crabs, to hide. Long-legged birds also wade through mud and water, looking for food.

106

Coral reefs have been around for at least 230 million years. They are among the oldest ecosystems in the world. Despite their great age, coral reefs do not appear to have changed very much in this time.

◀ The warm waters around mangrove roots are a perfect place for soft tree corals to grow.

Coral animals

107 Coral polyps are the little animals that build reefs. Their soft bodies are like rubber tubes with an opening at their centre. This is the mouth, which is surrounded by rows of tentacles. Each tentacle is equipped with stingers called cnidocytes (say nido-sites).

108 Coral polyps have a special relationship with tiny life-forms called zooxanthellae (say zoo-zan-thell-ee). These are plant-like algae that live inside a polyp's body, providing it with some of the food it needs to grow. In return, the polyps provide the algae with a safe place to live. Zooxanthellae need sunlight to survive, so they live inside a polyp's tentacles, where light can reach them.

◀ Cup corals are a non reef-building species that use their tentacles to catch prey. Coral polyps are in the same animal family as jellyfish and sea anemones, and are known as 'cnidarians' (say nid-air-ee-ans).

109 Sea animals do not always go looking for food. Coral polyps cannot move around, so they grab whatever food comes their way, using their tentacles. When a tentacle touches something edible, a tiny stinger springs out and pierces the prey's skin. The tentacles draw the prey into the polyp's mouth.

▶ Coral polyps have simple bodies. Inside, there is a large stomach, or gut. A tough rock-like skeleton grows outside.

Zooxanthellae

Chidocytes
(stinging cells)

Mouth

Tentacles

Stomach

Calcium carbonate
(stony skeleton)

110 Soft-bodied corals protect themselves by growing hard cases.

These cases are made from calcium carbonate, a tough substance that turns into stone over time. Each case is cup-shaped, and the polyp grows inside it. As new polyps develop, they build on top of one another – this is how the reef grows.

1. Planula searches for a place to settle

2. Planula attaches to a hard surface

111 Adult polyps are stuck in stony cups, but young polyps can swim.

A young polyp is called a planula and it is covered in tiny hairs that help it move through the water. It may float around for days or weeks until it finds a hard surface to attach itself to, and grow into an adult.

3. Polyp begins to grow a stony cup

▼ Polyps can reproduce in two ways. An egg can grow into a planula, or an adult can make a bud, which grows into a twin of itself.

4. Coral colony begins to grow through 'budding'

Hard and soft

112 There are two main types of coral — hard coral and soft coral. Hard coral polyps are reef-builders — they use calcium carbonate to build strong structures around themselves. Soft corals are bendy, and often live alongside their stony cousins.

113 Warm water reefs can look like colourful gardens. Corals grow in many unusual shapes, appearing like bushes, trees and mushrooms. The shape of coral depends upon the type of polyp that lives within it, and its position on the reef.

114 Some corals are easy to identify because they look just like their name. Brain corals, for example, look like brains. They grow very slowly and can reach the size of a boulder. Staghorn coral is one of the fastest-growing types, and it is an important reef-builder, especially in shallow waters. Each staghorn polyp can live for around ten years, and will not reproduce until it reaches at least three years old.

▼ Corals are different shapes and sizes. The way each coral grows depends on the type of polyps that live inside the rocky structures.

Elkhorn coral

Staghorn coral

Brain coral

Mushroom coral

115 Not all coral polyps live together in colonies. Some types live alone in the Southern Ocean, near the Antarctic, where temperatures rarely creep above a chilly 6°C. Little is known about solitary corals, but it is thought they are sensitive to water temperature.

Lettuce coral

Sea fan

Sea whip

Soft tree coral

Ancient reefs

116 Corals haven't changed much over the last few hundred million years. Coral polyps that lived at the same time as the dinosaurs, around 100 million years ago, are very similar to those alive today. The oldest coral on the Great Barrier Reef, Australia, is called porites. It is around 1000 years old.

117 Throughout time, extinctions (the dying out of a particular type of animal or plant) have occurred. The largest mass extinction happened around 250 million years ago. Many reef-building corals died out, to be replaced by other types that evolved thousands, or even millions, of years later.

▼ This is how a coral reef might have looked around 390 million years ago.

CORAL REEF KEY

1. Giant horn corals grew to one metre long
2. Shelled creatures with tentacles are related to today's octopuses
3. Crinoids grew long stems and a ring of feathery 'arms' around their mouths
4. Corals grew in large colonies, as they still do today

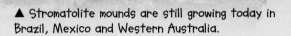

▲ Stromatolite mounds are still growing today in Brazil, Mexico and Western Australia.

118 **The oldest reefs were laid down more than 500 million years ago.** They were made of mounds, called stromatolites, that were created by tiny life-forms called cyanobacteria. Over millions of years, the mounds joined together to make ancient reefs.

▲ Coral colonies can harden and turn into stone over time. They are known as fossils.

119 **Over millions of years, coral reefs can turn into a type of stone, called limestone.** Scientists know about extinct reef animals by looking at limestones and the preserved remains of animals within them. These remains are called fossils and scientists can study them to understand how the Earth, animals and plants have changed over time.

120 **The sites of some ancient coral reefs have become land.** The Marshall Islands lie in the centre of the Pacific Ocean, near the Equator (the midway point between the North and South poles). The islands are made of limestone, and when scientists drilled deep down into the rock, they discovered that the oldest parts of the reefs there grew 50 million years ago.

Where in the world?

121 Warm water coral reefs may be packed with life, but they only cover around 284,000 square kilometres of the Earth's surface. If you put them all together, they would still only take up the same room as a small country, such as New Zealand.

122 Coral polyps are choosy about where they grow. This is because the zooxanthellae that live with them need warmth and light to turn the sun's energy into food. They are most likely to grow in seas and oceans within a region called the tropics, which is between the Tropic of Cancer and the Tropic of Capricorn.

◄ Damselfish and sea anemones are just two of the many animals that live on the Indian Ocean reefs.

Tropic of Cancer

RED SEA

▲ Blue-spotted stingrays hunt their prey among the Red Sea corals.

Coral Triangle

Equator

INDIAN OCEAN

Gr
Ba
R

123 The Coral Triangle is an enormous region that stretches across the seas around Indonesia, Malaysia and Papua New Guinea. It contains some of the world's most precious reefs, and is home to 3000 species of fish and 20 species of mammals, including dugongs, whales and dolphins.

Tropic of Capricorn

◄ A pink porcelain crab rests on a hard coral near Malaysia, in the Coral Triangle.

QUIZ
Which of these are oceans, and which are seas?
Atlantic   Mediterranean
Caribbean   Indian
Pacific   Coral

Answers:
Atlantic, Pacific and Indian are oceans. Caribbean, Mediterranean and Coral are seas.

124

Dirty water is no good to coral polyps. They prefer clear water, without the tiny particles of dirt, mud or sand that prevent light from reaching the seabed. Reefs don't grow near river mouths, or in areas where dirt is washed from the land into the sea. Polyps are even fussy about the amount of salt dissolved in the ocean water around them.

◄ Pygmy seahorses live in the warm coral waters of the western Pacific Ocean.

Hawaiian reefs

◄ The Hawaiian reef fish Humuhumunukunukuapua'a is a type of triggerfish, and makes pig-like snorting sounds if threatened.

ATLANTIC OCEAN

PACIFIC OCEAN

CARIBBEAN SEA

Mesoamerican Reef

125

Sunlight cannot pass through water as easily as it can pass through air. As zooxanthellae need light, their coral polyps only grow in water with a maximum depth of around 11 metres – although this varies depending on how clean the water is. This explains why warm water coral reefs grow near the land, where the water is shallow.

ORAL SEA

▲ The Caribbean reef octopus feeds at night, and eats fish and shelled animals.

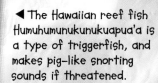

◄ Giant clams live in coral reefs around the South Pacific and Indian Oceans.

SOUTHERN OCEAN

Types of reef

126 There are three main types of coral reef. Fringing reefs are the most common. They grow on the edges of land that are underwater, often with little or no gap in between the reef and dry land. Barrier reefs also grow where land meets the ocean, but they are separated from the land by a stretch of water, called a lagoon. Atolls are circular reefs with a lagoon in the centre.

① When coral grows around an island's coasts, a fringing reef develops.

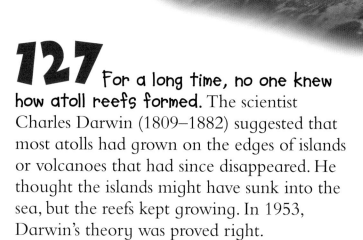
Island   Reef

127 For a long time, no one knew how atoll reefs formed. The scientist Charles Darwin (1809–1882) suggested that most atolls had grown on the edges of islands or volcanoes that had since disappeared. He thought the islands might have sunk into the sea, but the reefs kept growing. In 1953, Darwin's theory was proved right.

② The island drops, or the sea rises, and the coral becomes a barrier reef.

Island   Lagoon   Reef

I DON'T BELIEVE IT!
Coral polyps don't always make good neighbours. If space is short, the polyps from one coral might start to eat the polyps from a neighbouring one, or sting them to death.

128
Patch reefs form in shallow water and their tops are only visible at low tide. They are usually round or oval in shape and their outer edges are ringed by coral sand leading to beds of sea grass.

129
Bank reefs often grow in lines, or in semi-circles. They have large buttress zones (the area of a reef that faces the sea) with ridges of tough coral that grow out into it. Elkhorn coral grows here because it is able to withstand strong waves.

130
The Maldives are coral islands in the Indian Ocean. As they are built from coral, most land is no more than 1.5 metres above sea level. People have been living in the Maldives for more than 2000 years. There is little soil on the islands so few plants, other than coconut palms, grow well. Local people have survived by fishing and, more recently from tourism.

③ When there is no longer any sign of the island the reef is called an atoll.

Reef   Lagoon

Zones of the reef

131 Coral reefs can grow so large that it is possible to see them from outer space. Yet it is only the outer parts of a reef that are alive. The parts beneath the surface are dead, made up from the billions of stony cups that once housed living coral polyps.

Reef flat zone

Reef crest

Fore reef zo

Lagoon zone

Back reef

Buttress zo

Sea grasses

Sea turtle

Black sea urchins

Small brain coral

Plate coral

Stingray

Starfish

Elkhorn coral

▶ This diagram shows the zones of a barrier reef. A lagoon forms close to the land, and the reef stretches down to an area called the continental shelf into the deeper sea.

132 The part of a reef that is closest to land is called a reef flat. It is difficult for polyps to grow well here because of the effect of the tides, which may leave the coral exposed to air for too long, and because the water can become too salty. The reef flat is home to many types of animals that scuttle around between sea grasses, dig into the soft mud, or stick to the old, dead stony structures.

133 Most corals grow on the sides of the reef that face the sea and wind. This area is known as the fore reef and it is warmed by ocean currents. The corals here grow upwards and outwards, building up layers over thousands of years. Below the fore reef is a collection of old coral material that has broken off and fallen to the seafloor. The highest part of the fore reef is the crest – the polyps that live here must be able to survive strong waves and winds.

134 The fore reef is divided into three parts. At the bottom, plate-shaped corals grow where there is less light. As they grow they spread out to reach the sunlight. Nearby, fan corals are stretched in front of the water currents that flow towards them. In the middle part larger, mound-shaped corals grow and near the crest, long-fingered strong corals, such as staghorn, appear.

135 Further out to sea, a reef develops a buttress zone. Here, large spurs or clumps of coral grow, breaking up the waves and absorbing some of their impact before they hit the rest of the reef. This is the area where sharks and barracudas are most likely to swim. Beyond the buttress zone lies the reef wall, which forms in a deeper part of the sea.

Deep reef zone

Bottlenose dolphins

Sea goldies

Sea whip

Sea fan

I DON'T BELIEVE IT!
Coral reefs are very slow growers. A reef can grow about 10 centimetres a year if the conditions are just right – how much have you grown in the last year?

Maze coral

Tube sponge

Butterfly fish

Wobbegong shark

Barracudas

Dead coral bedrock

Lettuce coral

Star coral

Whitetip reef shark

Cold water corals

136 In the cold, dark ocean waters, coral reefs lay hidden for thousands of years. A few of these deep sea reefs were found about 250 years ago, but it has recently been discovered that in fact, there are more cold water reefs than warm water ones.

BIG BUILDERS

Find out about some other animal architects. Use the Internet or the library to discover how bees, termites and sociable weaver birds work together to build structures.

137 Cold water corals live in waters between 200 and 1500 metres deep. The largest cold water coral reef is more than 40 kilometres long and up to 3 kilometres wide. Just like warm water corals, these deep sea reefs are home to a large range of animals, many of which live nowhere else on Earth.

▼ A cold water reef grows in the chilly waters north of Scotland. Visible are dead man's fingers coral (1), a jewel anemone (2) and a common sea urchin (3).

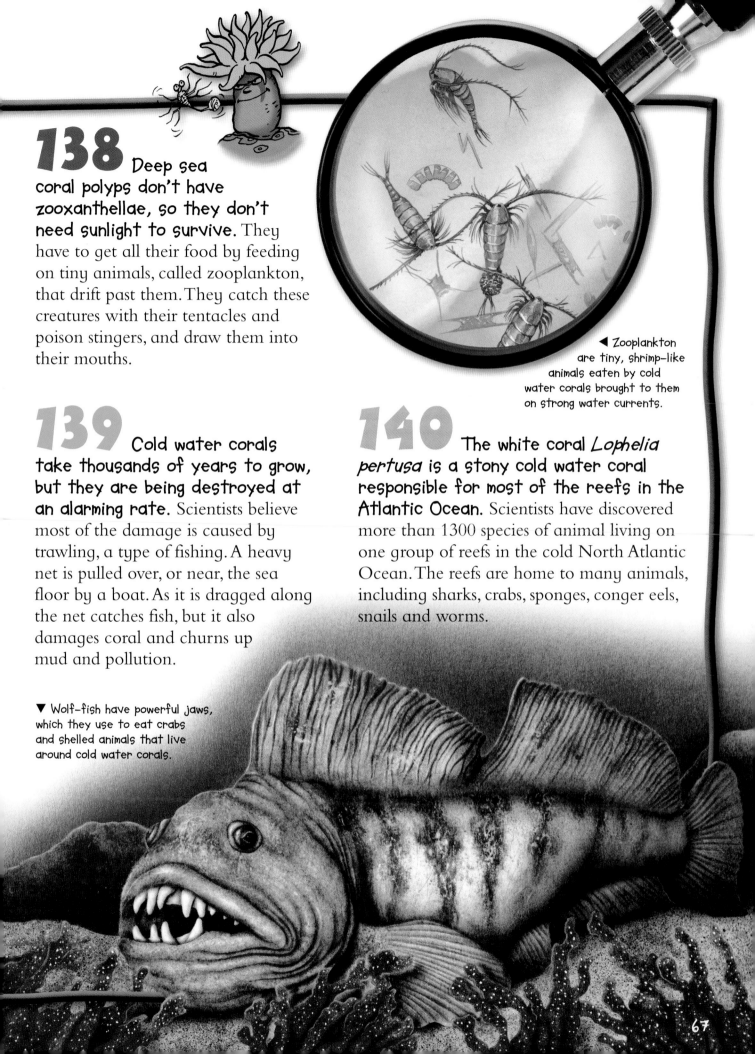

138
Deep sea coral polyps don't have zooxanthellae, so they don't need sunlight to survive. They have to get all their food by feeding on tiny animals, called zooplankton, that drift past them. They catch these creatures with their tentacles and poison stingers, and draw them into their mouths.

◀ Zooplankton are tiny, shrimp-like animals eaten by cold water corals brought to them on strong water currents.

139
Cold water corals take thousands of years to grow, but they are being destroyed at an alarming rate. Scientists believe most of the damage is caused by trawling, a type of fishing. A heavy net is pulled over, or near, the sea floor by a boat. As it is dragged along the net catches fish, but it also damages coral and churns up mud and pollution.

▼ Wolf-fish have powerful jaws, which they use to eat crabs and shelled animals that live around cold water corals.

140
The white coral *Lophelia pertusa* is a stony cold water coral responsible for most of the reefs in the Atlantic Ocean. Scientists have discovered more than 1300 species of animal living on one group of reefs in the cold North Atlantic Ocean. The reefs are home to many animals, including sharks, crabs, sponges, conger eels, snails and worms.

The Great Barrier Reef

141 The Great Barrier Reef, on the north-east coast of Australia, is possibly the largest structure ever built by animals. It covers an area of the Coral Sea that extends for more than 2000 kilometres and it took around 18 million years for the reef to grow to this enormous size.

142 It may look like one giant structure, but the Great Barrier Reef is really made up of around 3000 smaller reefs and 1000 islands. Although coral has grown in this region for millions of years the barrier reef only formed at the end of the last Ice Age, around 10,000 years ago.

◄ When leafy seadragons hide among seaweed they become almost invisible.

143 The Great Barrier Reef was not studied by scientists until the 18th century. British explorer James Cook (1728–1779) sailed his ship, HMS *Endeavour*, onto the reef in June 1770, and his crew had to spend six weeks repairing the damage to their craft. Ever since, explorers and scientists have been studying the structure of the reef and its wildlife.

▼ Dugongs are air-breathing animals that swim around the reef, grazing on sea grasses.

144 In 1975, the Great Barrier Reef Marine Park was set up to protect the reef. The area is home to an enormous variety of living things – there are 5000 species of molluscs, 1500 species of fish, 400 species of coral, 200 species of birds, 125 species of sharks, rays and skates, 30 species of whales, dolphins and porpoises, 14 species of sea snakes and six species of marine turtles!

▶ Groups, or shoals, of sweetlips swim around the Great Barrier Reef.

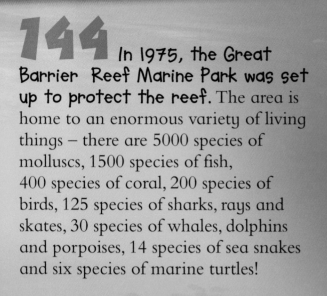

QUIZ

Can you add up all the numbers of species listed in fact 144, from molluscs to turtles? Check your answer with a calculator.

Answer:
5000 + 1500 + 400 + 200 +125 + 30 + 14 + 6 = 7275.

145 Native people and nearby islanders from the Torres Strait have fished in the Coral Sea for more than 60,000 years. They are known as the Traditional Owners of the Great Barrier Reef. The areas of the reef that they used in the practice of their ancient lifestyles are called the sea country. Traditional Owners work to preserve their ancient connection to the Great Barrier Reef.

◀ Like many sea snakes, olive sea snakes have a poisonous bite.

69

Caribbean coral

146 The world's second largest coral reef protects people from the effects of hurricanes (violent storms). It is called the Mesoamerican Reef, and it lies in the Caribbean Sea, west of the Atlantic Ocean.

147 Large areas of mangrove forest grow at the land's edge, behind the reef. Together, the mangroves and the corals create a barrier that slows down the hurricane-force storms that often batter the Caribbean coastlines. Mangrove roots help to bind the fragile shoreline, and stop rain and river water from washing too much dirt towards the coral. They also act as nurseries for young reef fish.

▶ Bottlenose dolphins visit the reefs but they also swim out into the open ocean.

▼ There are more than 500 species of fish in the Caribbean reefs, including the pretty queen angelfish.

148 The Mesoamerican reef is 225 million years old, 1127 kilometres long and home to more than 65 types of stony coral. There are also 350 species of mollusc, and 500 types of fish, including whale sharks. These gentle giants, which are the largest fish in the world, cruise the crystal-clear waters looking for tiny animals to scoop into their enormous mouths.

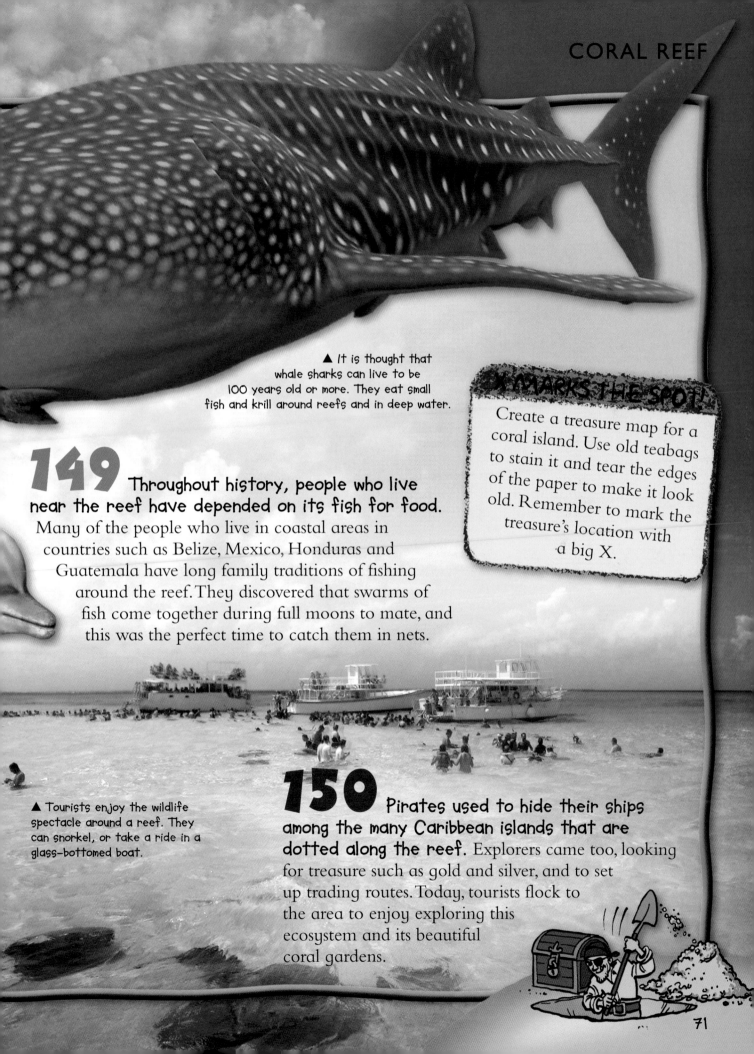

▲ It is thought that whale sharks can live to be 100 years old or more. They eat small fish and krill around reefs and in deep water.

X MARKS THE SPOT!
Create a treasure map for a coral island. Use old teabags to stain it and tear the edges of the paper to make it look old. Remember to mark the treasure's location with a big X.

149 Throughout history, people who live near the reef have depended on its fish for food. Many of the people who live in coastal areas in countries such as Belize, Mexico, Honduras and Guatemala have long family traditions of fishing around the reef. They discovered that swarms of fish come together during full moons to mate, and this was the perfect time to catch them in nets.

▲ Tourists enjoy the wildlife spectacle around a reef. They can snorkel, or take a ride in a glass-bottomed boat.

150 Pirates used to hide their ships among the many Caribbean islands that are dotted along the reef. Explorers came too, looking for treasure such as gold and silver, and to set up trading routes. Today, tourists flock to the area to enjoy exploring this ecosystem and its beautiful coral gardens.

Islands of fire

151 **The coral reefs of Hawaii are unlike any others found on Earth.** They have formed around a string of islands, called an archipelago, that developed when volcanoes erupted in the middle of the Pacific Ocean. Hawaii is about 3200 kilometres from any large land mass, which means these are the world's most isolated group of islands.

152 **Around one-quarter of the animals and plants that live on Hawaiian coral reefs are found nowhere else.** Algae, which are seaweeds, thrive in this area – especially the stony seaweeds that help to bind reefs together and make them stronger. Algae are important because they take carbon dioxide from the air and expel oxygen, the gas that animals such as polyps need to breathe.

▼ Enormous humpback whales use the waters around Hawaii as nurseries. They stay here with their young until it is time to swim north.

I DON'T BELIEVE IT!

Huge humpback whales feed on tiny krill, which are shrimp-like creatures. They don't feed in the winter, so at this time of year the krill have nothing to fear.

▲▶ Hawaiian corals (1) have grown on old lava that has cooled and turned to stone (2).

153 Volcanoes began to erupt in this area around 70 million years ago, and they are still active today. As lava cooled and turned to stone, corals began to grow on their edges. The first polyps must have arrived as free-swimming planulas, probably from other Pacific coral reefs.

154 Around 10,000 endangered humpback whales visit Hawaii every year. They arrive at the warm tropical waters in the winter, after swimming all the way from their feeding grounds in Alaska. While in Hawaii, the whales give birth to their young, and care for them. They can be seen swimming, playing and even battling with one another around the coral reefs.

◀ Green turtles lay their eggs on Hawaiian beaches because the reefs protect them from storms and waves.

155 The islanders of Hawaii set up a marine park in 1967, to protect the reef ecosystem. In 1956 an enormous channel, more than 60 metres wide, was blasted into the coral using dynamite to make way for a new telephone cable. The coral is now protected by law.

◀ A bobtail squid can produce light in its belly, which helps it hunt at night. The light is produced by bacteria that live on the squid.

A carnival of colour

156 Some animals stay on the sea floor, or hide in cracks in the coral reef, but others dart, dive and dazzle their way through the clear waters. Coral reef animals often use the colours of their shells or skins to help them lurk unseen in the shadows, or to warn other animals to stay away. When an animal uses colour to hide, it is said to be camouflaged.

157 Coral fish come in beautiful patterns and brilliant colours. Good looks are important for their survival – red colours appear dark in water, stripes provide camouflage and spots can confuse predators. Blue and yellow fish look bright to us, but they are hidden on the reef. The way sunlight is reflected off coral reefs affects the appearance of blues and yellows, making them blend in with the background.

▲▼ Coral fish come in many different colours and patterns such as the coral trout (top), regal angelfish (middle) and blue tang fish (below).

158 Squid and cuttlefish create flashes of colour. These soft-bodied molluscs can change their colours in an instant to hide or attract prey towards them. They can produce skin colours of red, yellow, orange, brown and black – and can even create patterns, such as zebra stripes, on their skin.

◀ Sea slugs are brightly coloured to warn predators that they are very poisonous.

159 Land slugs are slimy and often dull in colour, but coral reef slugs are bizarre, beautiful animals. Sea slugs, also called nudibranchs, don't have shells, but they do have soft, feathery gills on their backs, which help them to breathe in water. Some nudibranchs are small, but the largest ones can grow to 30 centimetres long.

160 The stripes, spines and bright colours of a lionfish spell danger to other coral creatures. These ocean fish hunt other fish, shrimp and sea anemones. When they are threatened they react with lightning speed. Lionfish have spines on their bodies that carry deadly venom, which they raise and plunge into a predator's flesh.

▼ Lionfish hide among rocks in the daytime, and only come out at night to hunt for food. They have been known to threaten divers.

GO FISH!
Choose your favourite colourful coral fish from this book and copy it onto a large piece of paper or card. Use different materials, such as paints, tissue paper, buttons and foil to show the colours and patterns.

On the attack

161 Animals need energy to survive, and they get that energy from food. Some reef animals graze on seaweeds and corals, but others hunt and kill to feed. Hunting animals are called predators, and their victims are called prey.

▶ When sharks, such as these lemon sharks, sense blood or food they move with speed to attack their prey.

162 Some coral sharks aren't aggressive and divers can feed them by hand. Bull sharks are not so relaxed around humans. They have been known to attack divers and swimmers around reefs. Sharks are drawn to coral reefs because of the thousands of fish on the reef but finding prey is not always easy when there are so many good hiding places.

163 Cone shells look harmless, but their appearance is deceptive. These sea snails crawl around reefs looking for prey such as worms, molluscs and fish. They fire venom-filled darts to paralyze their prey. The dart remains attached to the cone shell, so it can draw its victim back to its body and devour it.

◀ This small animal cannot protect itself from an attack by a deadly cone shell.

164 Sea anemones and jellyfish have stingers to attack their prey, just like their coral cousins. Soft-bodied sea anemones are usually quite small and they stay attached to the sea floor, or coral, and wait for water currents to bring food their way. Jellyfish have tentacles that can stretch for many metres, hanging below their bodies. Jellyfish can swim, or they are carried along by the sea's currents.

165 Mantis shrimps are mighty crustaceans. They punch or spear their prey, using such incredible force and speed that they are regarded as one of the most powerful animals in the world for their size. These small animals are common in Australian coral reefs and parts of the Indo-Pacific reef system.

▼ A blue-ringed octopus is only 20 centimetres long but its saliva contains poison that is strong enough to kill a human.

▲ Box jellyfish have such deadly stings that beaches are often closed in Australia when they are present in the water.

I DON'T BELIEVE IT!
Mantis shrimps are powerful punchers. They surprise their prey by hitting out at speeds of 240 metres per second.

Living together

166 **The animals and plants that live on coral reefs need each other to survive.** The close relationship between some animals is known as 'symbiosis'. Sometimes these partnerships give benefits to both animals, but at other times one animal gains little.

167 **Coral polyps and their zooxanthellae are best buddies.** Each zooxanthellae is made of just one cell. Like green plants, zooxanthellae make food using sunlight, water and carbon dioxide – a gas that is in the air. This process is called photosynthesis. The food they make is eaten by the polyps. Because they need sunlight to grow, zooxanthellae live inside a polyp's tentacles where light can reach them.

▼ Clownfish can hide among the stinging tentacles of a sea anemone without getting stung.

▲ Remora fish use other animals – such as this green turtle – to hitch a ride and find food.

I DON'T BELIEVE IT!

Boxer crabs use stinging sea anemones like boxing gloves. They wave them at any predators who get too close!

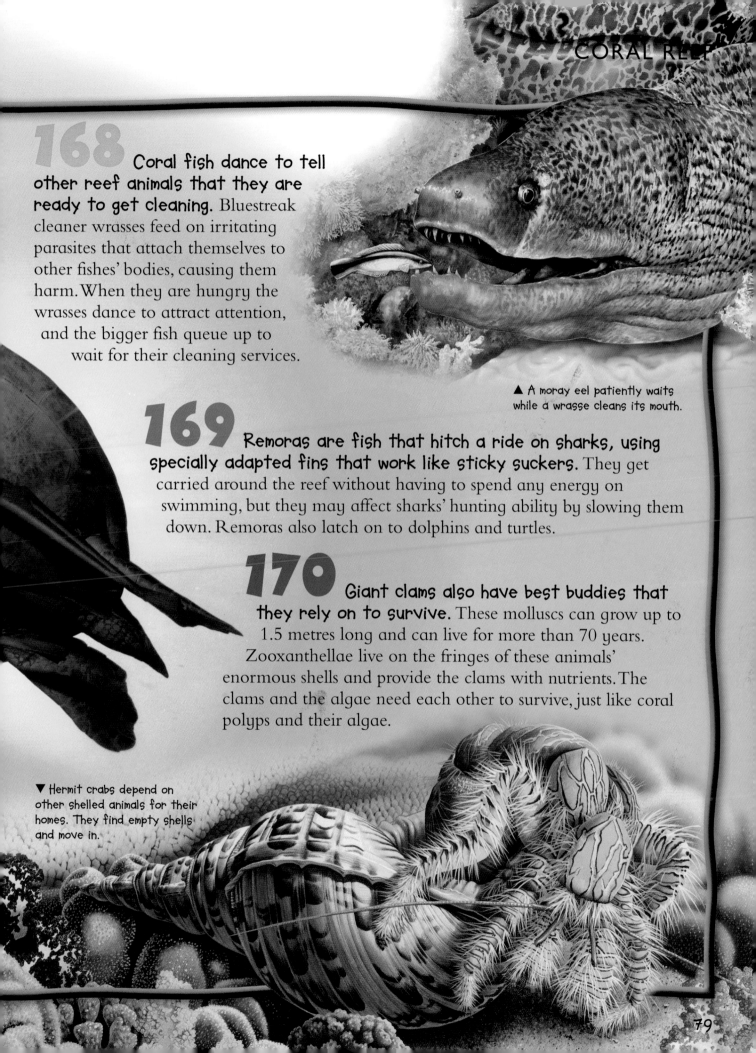

168 Coral fish dance to tell other reef animals that they are ready to get cleaning. Bluestreak cleaner wrasses feed on irritating parasites that attach themselves to other fishes' bodies, causing them harm. When they are hungry the wrasses dance to attract attention, and the bigger fish queue up to wait for their cleaning services.

▲ A moray eel patiently waits while a wrasse cleans its mouth.

169 Remoras are fish that hitch a ride on sharks, using specially adapted fins that work like sticky suckers. They get carried around the reef without having to spend any energy on swimming, but they may affect sharks' hunting ability by slowing them down. Remoras also latch on to dolphins and turtles.

170 Giant clams also have best buddies that they rely on to survive. These molluscs can grow up to 1.5 metres long and can live for more than 70 years. Zooxanthellae live on the fringes of these animals' enormous shells and provide the clams with nutrients. The clams and the algae need each other to survive, just like coral polyps and their algae.

▼ Hermit crabs depend on other shelled animals for their homes. They find empty shells and move in.

Night on the reef

171 As the Sun sets over the ocean, coral reefs change. Polyps emerge from their cups and unfurl their tentacles, producing a range of colours and movements. Creatures that were active in daylight rest in dark crevices, while others emerge to feed in the dark.

172 Coral animals that come out at night are described as nocturnal. They often have senses that help them to detect movement, light, sound and chemicals in the inky-blue seas. Octopuses have superb night vision and long tentacles that they use to probe cracks in the reef, searching for food.

◄ Corals are nocturnal and are most active at night.

173 Coral reef spiny lobsters march through the night. At the end of the summer 100,000 of them set off on a long journey. Walking in single file towards deeper, darker water, they can travel up to 50 kilometres every night to reach their breeding grounds.

▼ A Christmas tree worm buries its body deep inside a coral. Only its two feeding tentacles, which look like trees, are visible.

◀ Red soldierfish have unusually large eyes, which help them to see in the dark.

175 **Divers can swim with giant stingrays at night.** These enormous fish can measure up to 2 metres across and they often glide through the water in groups, gently flapping their 'wings' to move silently and swiftly. Stingrays do not need light to hunt because they are able to detect the electricity inside other animals' bodies, and use this information to find prey such as clams and oysters.

174 **Fireworms are rarely seen in the day.** They live under rocks and have venom-filled spines on their backs, giving them a furry appearance. During the summer adult worms emerge once at night, during a full moon, to mate. The females produce a green glow that attracts the males in the dark water.

▼ Mandarin fish rest during the day, but come out of their rocky shelters at night to hunt and feed.

Light organ

▲ Most flashlight fish live in deep waters, where their ability to make light is most useful. Some types, however, swim into coral waters at night.

Relying on reefs

176 Millions of people rely on coral reefs for their survival. These ecosystems not only support fish and other animals, they also protect coastal regions from damage by storms and wave action.

▲ The people from this fishing village in Borneo depend on the reef for food.

177 There are around 500 types of seaweeds living on the Great Barrier Reef alone. Seaweeds contain substances that are useful to humans. Agar comes from red seaweeds and is used to make desserts, or to thicken soups and ice cream. Alginates come from brown seaweeds and they are used to make cosmetics, thicken drinks and in the manufacture of paper and textiles.

178 Ecosystems that have a large range of living things are often used in medical science. Many species of animals and plants that live on reefs are being used in the search for new medicines that will cure illnesses. Substances in coral polyps are being used to develop treatments for some diseases, and to help rebuild broken bones.

179 People who live around reefs have traded in coral products for thousands of years. The harvesting of red and pink corals for jewellery has caused many people to worry that the coral may be driven to extinction. Jewellery makers are asked to only use a small amount of coral every year and to only take coral from places where it will be protected as it regrows.

▶ Collecting food, such as fish, and precious coral is a traditional way to survive in many places where reefs grow.

180 Coral reefs help to support local communities through tourism. Millions of people flock to the world's reefs to enjoy nature's underwater spectacle. The money they spend there helps support local people, who provide accommodation, food and equipment. Reefs are worth much more alive than dead. While one shark could be killed and sold for food, it is worth at least one hundred times more alive as an attraction to reef tourists.

▼ A trained guide shows tourists the delights of the Great Barrier Reef. 'Ecotourism' allows visitors to enjoy the reef without damaging it.

Underwater explorers

181 **Exploring a reef is a magical experience.** Bathed in warm, blue water, a diver can swim among thousands of fish that dart around the coral. As schools of small, silvery fish flash past, smaller groups of predator fish follow – fast and alert in the chase.

182 **People have been fascinated by coral reefs for thousands of years.** They have enjoyed watching reef wildlife, but they have also explored in search of food and building materials. Since coral reefs grow in shallow, clear water swimmers can enjoy them without any special equipment. Snorkels allow swimmers to breathe while their faces are in water.

183 **The best way to explore a coral reef is to go underwater.** Scuba equipment allows a diver to swim and breathe below the water's surface. Using an oxygen tank, flippers and a face mask a diver can move carefully around a reef, watching the creatures or carrying out scientific studies.

▼ Special equipment allows divers to photograph underwater wildlife such as this Goliath grouper.

184

Scientists have been examining coral reefs for more than 300 years. There are many research centres and universities near large coral reefs, so scientists can collect information and learn about the reefs over many years. There are even underwater research laboratories, where scientists can study reefs close up for days at a time.

▼ Divers explore old reefs, but they also visit places where new reefs are forming on shipwrecks, to understand how they develop.

185

Exploring reefs is fascinating, but it can be dangerous too. Curious blacktip reef sharks may give a diver a warning nip, but a sting from a box jellyfish can be deadly. There are also poisonous sea snakes, octopuses, shellfish and fish.

Natural coral Killers

186 Some fish not only live on a reef, they eat it too. There are more than 130 types of fish, known as corallivores, that feed on corals. They eat the slimy mucus made by polyps, the polyps themselves and even their stony cups. They like eating polyps during their breeding season because they are full of juicy, tasty eggs.

▲ Most coral-eating fish are butterfly fish. They have small mouths that can nibble at polyps and their eggs.

▼ Parrotfish change their appearance throughout their lives — they change colour as they grow up!

187 Reef-killing creatures have different eating habits around the world. In some regions, the coral-eating fish remove so much of the reef that it does not appear to grow at all. Threadfin butterfly fish in the Indian Ocean munch through large amounts of coral, but those that live around the Great Barrier Reef never eat coral. Corallivores that live in Caribbean reefs can survive on other food, too.

188 Parrotfish are dazzling in their appearance, but deadly in their lifestyle. They dig at coral with their tough mouths, which are like beaks, and grind it up in their throats. This releases the zooxanthellae that are an important part of their diet. The stony parts of the coral pass through their bodies, coming out the other end as beautiful white sand.

▲ Crown-of-thorns starfish graze on corals, especially in places where the starfish's natural enemy, the trumpet shellfish, has disappeared.

189 The crown-of-thorns starfish is one of the world's most famous coral-killers. It is covered in spines and can have as many as 21 'arms'. This starfish eats coral by turning its mouth inside out and pouring strong juices over the polyps to dissolve their flesh. It prefers fast-growing corals over the slower-growing types. The starfish eat the polyps, but leave the stony structure behind.

190 In the 1980s, Caribbean black sea urchins, called diademas, were wiped out by a deadly disease. These sea urchins kept the reefs healthy by grazing on seaweeds. Once they had died, seaweeds took over the coral, using up space and blocking out light. Seaweed-eating fish were also struggling to survive because too many of them had been caught by fishermen. There was nothing left to control the growth of seaweed and so the coral ecosystem was changed, and may never return to its previous, healthy state.

I DON'T BELIEVE IT!
Sponges are boring animals — they bore right into coral reefs! These simple animals dig right into the middle of a reef, making it weaker and more likely to collapse in storms.

Reefs at risk

191 Coral reefs are fragile ecosystems that are under threat from humans. When they are stressed, coral polyps lose their zooxanthellae, and die. Once the polyps have died the coral structure that is left appears white, and is described as 'bleached'.

▼ If zooxanthellae leave the coral, the polyps die. Over time, other types of algae and bacteria grow over the bleached coral.

1. Healthy coral with zooxanthellae living in coral tissue

2. Zooxanthellae leave coral due to increased water temperatures

3. Algae cover the damaged coral

▶ Global warming, a rise in worldwide temperatures, is caused by the polluting effects of carbon dioxide. It is raising sea temperatures and is causing coral bleaching.

192
Pollution, such as human waste (sewage) and chemicals used in farming, kills coral. In some places, pipes carry sewage to the sea where it mixes with the seawater. Sewage contains substances that feed seaweeds but bleach corals. On land, chemicals are used on crops to help them grow or to kill pests, but they get carried out to sea by rainwater and rivers, where they damage the reef and its inhabitants.

193
Damage to nearby land causes reefs to die. When coastal areas are changed by building or digging, soil is loosened and makes its way into the sea. Soil and dirt in seawater make it cloudy and stop sunlight from reaching the zooxanthellae. The result is more coral bleaching.

▶ Coral is broken up and taken from the sea to be used as a building material.

194
Catching and killing fish adds to the bleaching of coral reefs. In some parts of the world, fishermen use destructive methods of fishing. They drop bombs in the water, which explode and kill whole schools of fish, turning coral to crumbs. They also use chemicals, such as cyanide.

195
Tourists enjoy reefs, but they also put them at risk. Visitors put pressure on local ecosystems because they need food, transport and places to stay – which means pollution, fishing and building. Some tourists damage reefs by standing on them or touching them, and by buying wildlife souvenirs such as coral jewellery.

SAVE OUR REEFS!
Make a poster to show the different ways coral reefs are being damaged and destroyed. Include a list of top tips for tourists to help them enjoy reefs safely without harming these ecosystems.

DEEP OCEAN

201 **Far down in the dark waters of the deep oceans lies a mysterious wilderness.** The deep ocean is a place without light, where the water pressure can crush human bones. Until modern times, people did not believe that anything could live here. Now scientists are discovering new creatures all the time, from colossal squid with huge eyes to giant worms that are 2 metres in length.

▶ Almost 2.5 kilometres below the surface of the ocean, an eelpout fish hides among giant tube worms and crabs at a hydrothermal vent. Only two people have been to the deepest part of the oceans, which is about 11 kilometres below the waves. In contrast, 12 human explorers have walked on the surface of the Moon, which is 384,400 kilometres from Earth.

The ocean zones

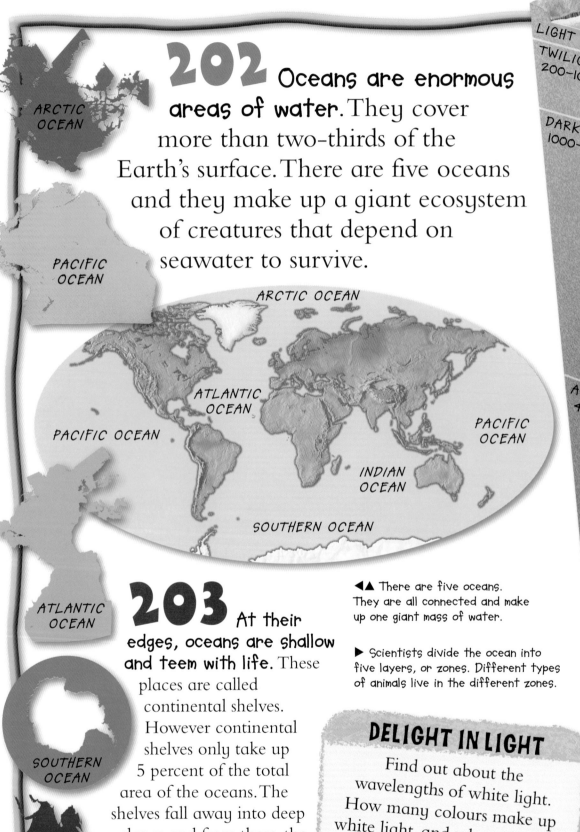

202 Oceans are enormous areas of water. They cover more than two-thirds of the Earth's surface. There are five oceans and they make up a giant ecosystem of creatures that depend on seawater to survive.

ARCTIC OCEAN

PACIFIC OCEAN

ATLANTIC OCEAN

INDIAN OCEAN

SOUTHERN OCEAN

ARCTIC OCEAN

PACIFIC OCEAN

ATLANTIC OCEAN

SOUTHERN OCEAN

INDIAN OCEAN

LIGHT ZONE 0–200 metres
Jellyfish

TWILIGHT ZONE 200–1000 metres

DARK ZONE 1000–4000 metres

Sea lily

ABYSSAL ZONE 4000–6000 metres

Tube worms

HADAL ZONE 6000–10,000 metres

203 At their edges, oceans are shallow and teem with life. These places are called continental shelves. However continental shelves only take up 5 percent of the total area of the oceans. The shelves fall away into deep slopes and from there, the seabed stretches out as dark, enormous plains.

◀▲ There are five oceans. They are all connected and make up one giant mass of water.

▶ Scientists divide the ocean into five layers, or zones. Different types of animals live in the different zones.

DELIGHT IN LIGHT
Find out about the wavelengths of white light. How many colours make up white light, and what are they? Find the answers by searching on the Internet with the keywords 'rainbow' and 'light'.

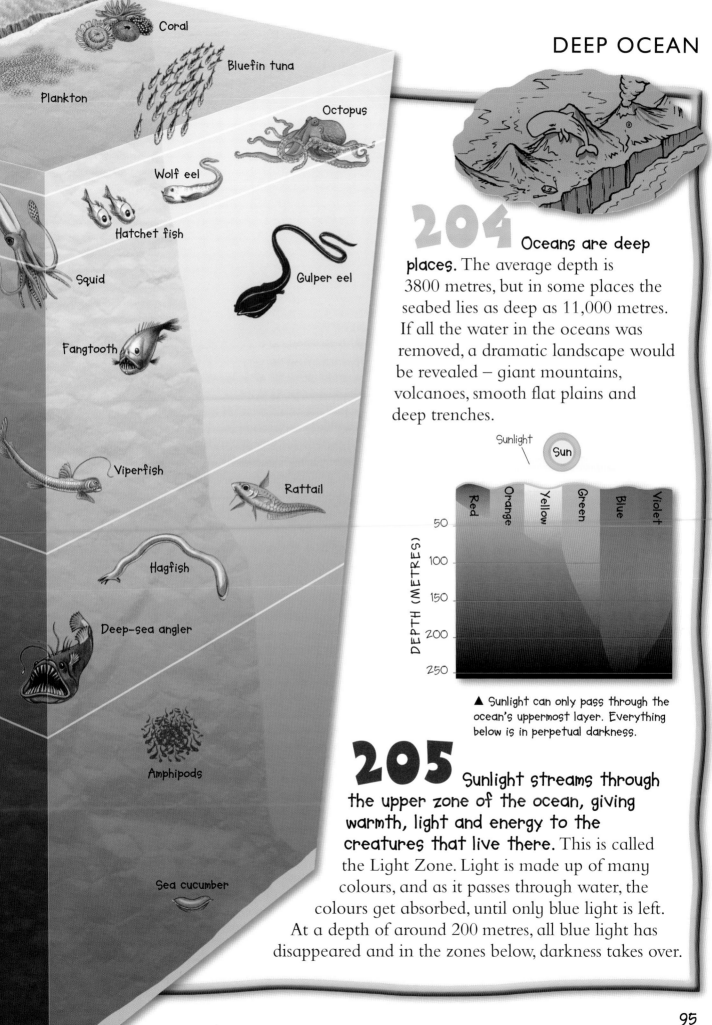

Coral

Plankton

Bluefin tuna

Octopus

Wolf eel

Hatchet fish

Squid

Gulper eel

Fangtooth

Viperfish

Rattail

Hagfish

Deep-sea angler

Amphipods

Sea cucumber

204 Oceans are deep places. The average depth is 3800 metres, but in some places the seabed lies as deep as 11,000 metres. If all the water in the oceans was removed, a dramatic landscape would be revealed – giant mountains, volcanoes, smooth flat plains and deep trenches.

Sunlight

Sun

DEPTH (METRES)

Red Orange Yellow Green Blue Violet

50

100

150

200

250

▲ Sunlight can only pass through the ocean's uppermost layer. Everything below is in perpetual darkness.

205 Sunlight streams through the upper zone of the ocean, giving warmth, light and energy to the creatures that live there. This is called the Light Zone. Light is made up of many colours, and as it passes through water, the colours get absorbed, until only blue light is left. At a depth of around 200 metres, all blue light has disappeared and in the zones below, darkness takes over.

In deep water

206 Living in water is nothing like living in air. The ocean is one of Earth's most remarkable habitats. Ocean water is constantly moving and changing. The creatures that live here have to cope without light, and the weight of many tonnes of water above them.

208 As you travel deeper into the ocean you will feel a great weight on your body. Water is 830 times denser than air, and it is very heavy. It is water's density that helps things to float, or stay buoyant. However, the further down you go, the more pressure the water forces on you.

Cold deep current

Warm surface current

◄ Cold water is denser than warm water, and it sinks to the ocean depths near the polar regions.

Deep water formation

Warm surface current

Cold deep current

◄ Water travels in currents around the world. The largest and deepest of these form a system called the global conveyor.

DEPTH (METRES)

0 — 1 atm
10 — 2 atm
20 — 3 atm
30 — 4 atm
40 — 5 atm

207 At the surface, wind creates waves and the Moon's gravitational pull causes tides. Further down, other forces are in action. Ocean water is continually moving, passing around the globe in giant streams called currents. If you were to get caught in one of these strong, deep currents, after 1000 years you would have journeyed all around the world!

► Water pressure is measured in atmospheres (atm). Pressure increases with depth, squashing the molecules of air in this balloon.

209

Although you will soon be cold, you may notice that the temperature of the water around you doesn't change much. Ocean water has great heat capacity, which means that it warms up slowly and cools down slowly too. It can hold on to its temperature about 4000 times better than air can.

▼ Many enormous animals, such as this basking shark, live in the ocean. The dense, salty seawater supports their great weight.

210

The good news is that you won't have to work hard to get food. If you stay still, it will float right past your nose. Because water is dense, tiny creatures and particles of food are suspended in it. Some sea creatures can wave tentacles to catch food, or just open their mouths as they swim!

◀ A magnified view of plankton, tiny animals and plants that float or swim in seawater. They often become food for bigger animals.

MAKING WATER HEAVY

You will need:
two identical cups containing the same amount of water   salt

Add salt to one of the cups and stir. Continue until no more salt will dissolve. Weigh both cups – the salty one should be heavier. Salty water is denser and heavier than fresh water.

▶ A beaker of ocean water may look dirty, but it is full of substances that are food for tiny organisms called phytoplankton.

211

You should never drink seawater. It has lots of minerals, called salts, dissolved in it. A single bath of seawater contains 2.8 kilograms of salts. Most of that is sodium chloride (common salt). Gases, such as oxygen and nitrogen are also dissolved in seawater.

Other elements 0.6%
Sodium 1%
Chloride 1.9%
Water 96.5%
Salt 3.5%

The Light Zone

212 The top 200 metres of the ocean is called the Light Zone. At the continental shelf, sunlight can reach all the way to the seabed. However within 10 metres of the water's surface, nearly all of the red parts of light have been absorbed, which means that many creatures appear dull in colour.

▲ The shiny scales on tuna fish reflect sunlight as they dart from side to side, to confuse their predators.

▶ Green turtles have to visit the surface to breathe air, then they dive to feed on marine plants.

213 Sunlight provides the energy for plants to grow. Marine plants such as seaweed need light in order to make food from carbon dioxide and water, in a process called photosynthesis. Plants also produce oxygen, the gas we breathe, and without it there would be no life in the oceans.

◀ Marine plants, including seaweed (shown here) and phytoplankton, are called algae.

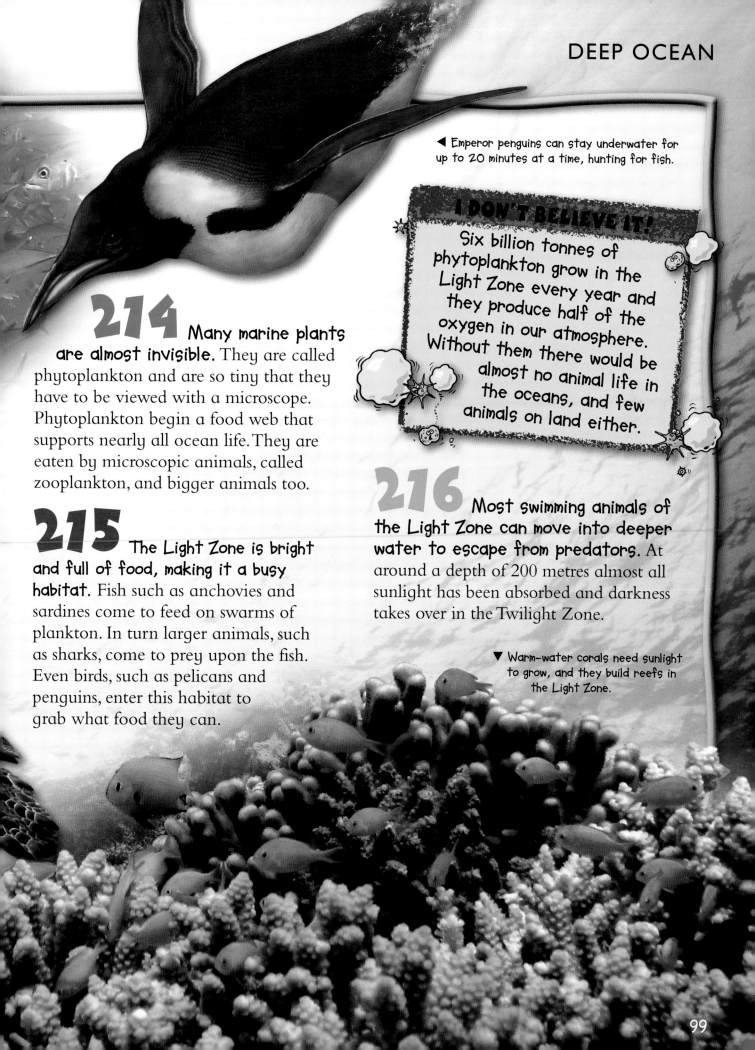

◀ Emperor penguins can stay underwater for up to 20 minutes at a time, hunting for fish.

I DON'T BELIEVE IT!

Six billion tonnes of phytoplankton grow in the Light Zone every year and they produce half of the oxygen in our atmosphere. Without them there would be almost no animal life in the oceans, and few animals on land either.

214 Many marine plants are almost invisible. They are called phytoplankton and are so tiny that they have to be viewed with a microscope. Phytoplankton begin a food web that supports nearly all ocean life. They are eaten by microscopic animals, called zooplankton, and bigger animals too.

215 The Light Zone is bright and full of food, making it a busy habitat. Fish such as anchovies and sardines come to feed on swarms of plankton. In turn larger animals, such as sharks, come to prey upon the fish. Even birds, such as pelicans and penguins, enter this habitat to grab what food they can.

216 Most swimming animals of the Light Zone can move into deeper water to escape from predators. At around a depth of 200 metres almost all sunlight has been absorbed and darkness takes over in the Twilight Zone.

▼ Warm-water corals need sunlight to grow, and they build reefs in the Light Zone.

The Twilight Zone

217 From a depth of 200 to 1000 metres lies the Twilight Zone. Just enough light reaches this zone for animals to see, and be seen by. Predators and prey battle it out in a constant fight for survival.

Siphuncle

Jaws

Brain

Tentacles

Funnel

Gills

Heart

Stomach

Digestive gland

Gonad

▲ A nautilus fills the chambers in its shell with water or gas by a tube called a siphuncle. Like octopuses and squid, a nautilus propels itself by pushing water out of its funnel.

218 Mighty sperm whales plunge into the Twilight Zone when they are hunting squid. They can dive to depths of 1000 metres and hold their breath for up to 90 minutes at a time. The deepest known dive of any sperm whale was 3000 metres, and the whale swam at a speed of 4 metres a second to get there!

219 The nautilus can swim, float and move up and down in the Twilight Zone. It lives in the outermost chamber of its shell, and its inner chambers are filled with gas or liquid. By pushing gas into the chambers, liquid is forced out and the nautilus becomes lighter – and floats up. When the gas is replaced with liquid, the nautilus sinks.

◄ Huge sperm whales are mammals, which means they have to return to the surface to breathe.

220 It is hard to see if your eyes are deep inside your head. Barreleye fish don't mind because they have see-through heads. They swim with their big, green eyes peering upwards. When the fish sees its prey, it flips its body upright and rotates its eyes in its head. This allows the fish to keep its prey in view while swimming up to grab it.

Eye

Mouth

Nostril

◄ A barreleye fish's eyes are very sensitive, which help it to spot its prey in low light.

▼ Comb jellies swim by beating rows of comb-like plates, which bend light rays to make colourful shimmers.

221 There are few hard surfaces to attach to, so animals in the Twilight Zone are mostly floaters and swimmers. Many have unusual shapes and their bodies are often soft and watery. Comb jellies are soft-bodied animals, but they can turn hard by contracting muscles. Some have long, sticky tentacles to grab prey.

▼ Sea pens anchor themselves to the seafloor in the Twilight Zone. They feed on plankton by catching it in their feathery branches.

TRUE OR FALSE?

1. Barreleye fish have see-through heads.
2. Sperm whales can breathe underwater.
3. Nautiluses swim using fins.
4. The Twilight Zone is pitch black.

Answers:
1. True 2. False 3. False 4. False

Monster of the deep

222 **Giant squid are monsters of the deep.** They can grow to 15 metres in length, including tentacles, which alone can grow to 12 metres. Their eyes are thought to be the largest of any animal. Each one is up to 40 centimetres in diameter!

223 **Little is known about these mysterious animals because they live in the Twilight Zone.** Giant squid can swim well, and with their good eyesight they can spot fishing nets and move swiftly away. Very few have ever been caught, and what is known about them has been revealed from dead specimens, or remains that have been found in the stomachs of sperm whales.

▶ Giant squid have a reputation as fearsome monsters. In fact, they are more likely to be gentle giants of the deep.

QUIZ

Put these animal giants in order of size, from largest to smallest:
African elephant
Hercules beetle
Blue whale   Giant squid

Answer:
Blue whale, giant squid,
African elephant, Hercules beetle

Teeth

Sucker

Tentacle

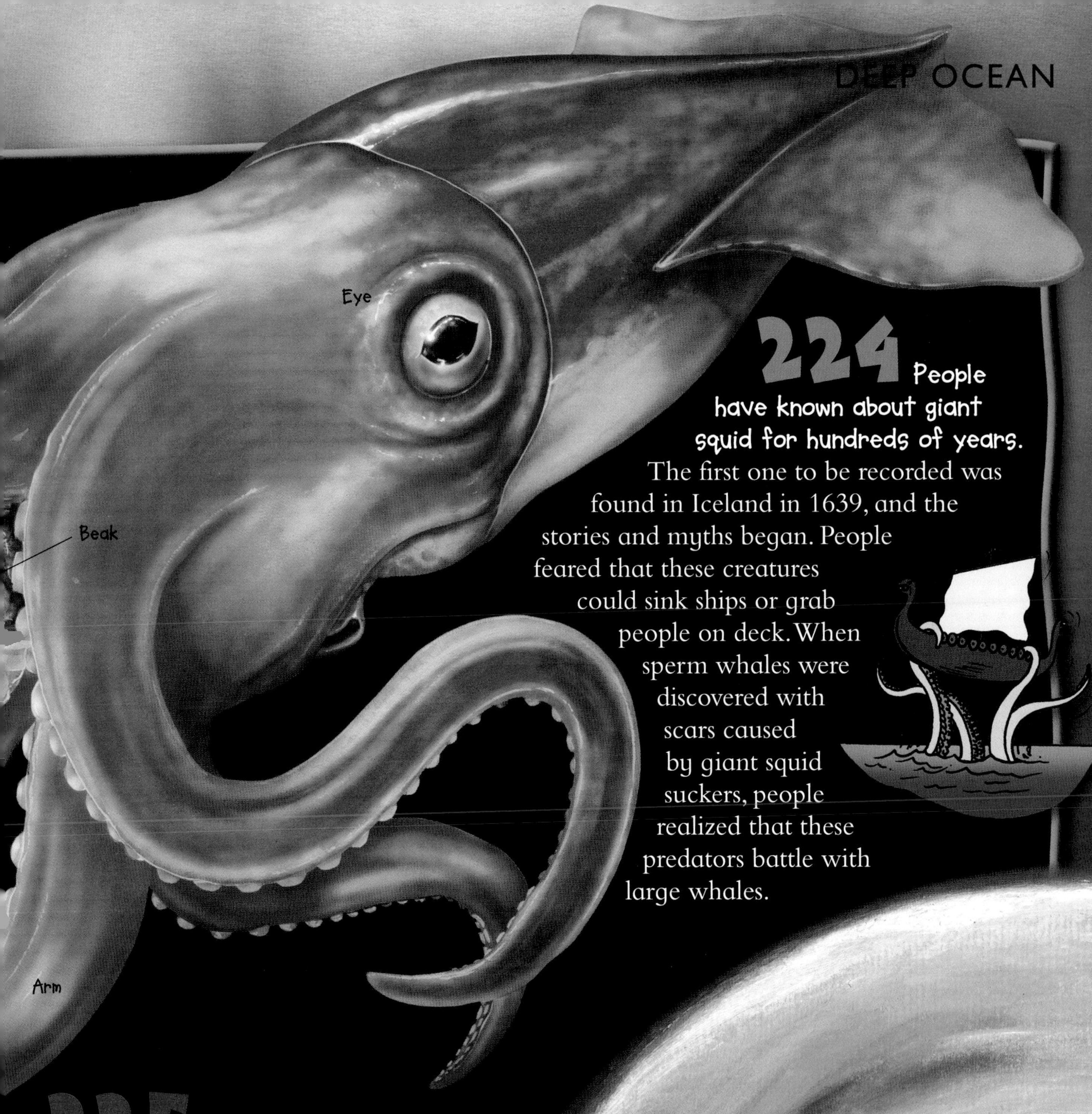

Eye

Beak

Arm

224 People have known about giant squid for hundreds of years. The first one to be recorded was found in Iceland in 1639, and the stories and myths began. People feared that these creatures could sink ships or grab people on deck. When sperm whales were discovered with scars caused by giant squid suckers, people realized that these predators battle with large whales.

225 **Giant squid are predators.** No one knows for sure how they live, but like other squid they probably hunt fish, octopuses and smaller squid. Their muscular tentacles are equipped with giant, toothed suckers that can grab hold of wriggly prey.

▶ The eye of a giant squid has a diameter bigger than a person's head.

The Dark Zone

226 Below 1000 metres absolutely no light can penetrate. So far from the Sun's rays, this habitat is intensely cold, and there is bone-crushing pressure from the enormous weight of water above. It is called the Dark Zone, and it extends to 4000 metres below the ocean's surface.

227 It snows in the Dark Zone! Billions of particles fall down towards the seabed, and this is called marine snow. This 'snow' is made up of droppings from animals above, and animals and plants that have died. Small flakes often collect together to become larger and heavier, drifting down up to 200 metres a day. Marine snow is an important source of food for billions of deep-sea creatures.

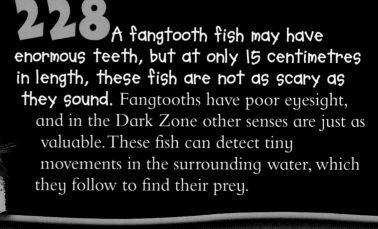

▲ Fierce-looking fangtooth fish can swim to depths of around 5000 metres, into the Abyssal Zone, when they follow their prey.

I DON'T BELIEVE IT!

The orange roughy lives in deep water where its colour appears black if any light reaches it. This is believed to be one of the longest living fish – one individual allegedly reached 149 years of age.

228 A fangtooth fish may have enormous teeth, but at only 15 centimetres in length, these fish are not as scary as they sound. Fangtooths have poor eyesight, and in the Dark Zone other senses are just as valuable. These fish can detect tiny movements in the surrounding water, which they follow to find their prey.

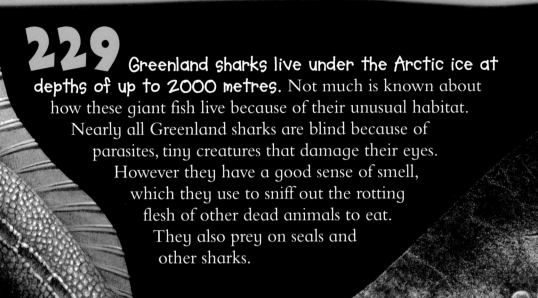

229 Greenland sharks live under the Arctic ice at depths of up to 2000 metres. Not much is known about how these giant fish live because of their unusual habitat. Nearly all Greenland sharks are blind because of parasites, tiny creatures that damage their eyes. However they have a good sense of smell, which they use to sniff out the rotting flesh of other dead animals to eat. They also prey on seals and other sharks.

▲ Greenland sharks can grow to 6 metres long. They live in the Arctic and often swim close to shore, but pose little threat to humans.

▼ Giant isopods are crustaceans that live in the Dark Zone. They are related to crabs, shrimps, lobsters and woodlice, and can reach a length of 35 centimetres. Isopods have long antennae that help them feel their way in the dark.

230 Giant isopods are peculiar crawling creatures that look like huge woodlice. Their bodies are protected by tough plates, and they can roll themselves up into a ball when they come under attack. Isopods live on the seabed, searching for soft-bodied animals to eat.

The Abyssal Zone

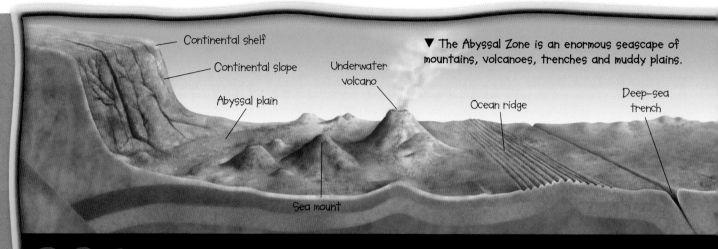

Continental shelf

Continental slope

Underwater volcano

Abyssal plain

Ocean ridge

Deep-sea trench

Sea mount

▼ The Abyssal Zone is an enormous seascape of mountains, volcanoes, trenches and muddy plains.

ABYSSAL ZONE

231 Below the Dark Zone is the Abyssal Zone, or abyss, which reaches from 4000 to 6000 metres. Where the continental slope ends, the sea floor stretches out in a giant plain. Around one-third of the seabed is in the Abyssal Zone.

232 The abyssal plains have mountains (called sea mounts), trenches and valleys. Many sea mounts are drowned volcanoes, and there may be 30,000 of them in the world's oceans. The sides of the mounts are sheer, which causes water to flow upwards in a process called upwelling. This flow of water brings nutrients to the area, and many animals live in these habitats.

233 Most waters of the Abyssal Zone contain little food. Animals rely on finding marine snow, which may take several months to fall from the surface, or hunting other deep-sea creatures. Many are scavengers, which means they only feed when they find food, such as the remains of other animals that have died. With a shortage of food, creatures here move around very little to save energy.

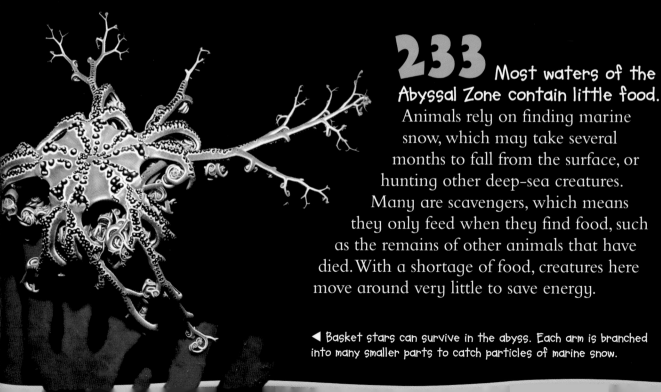

◄ Basket stars can survive in the abyss. Each arm is branched into many smaller parts to catch particles of marine snow.

▼ There are around 60 types of hagfish. They have eel-like bodies with four hearts, but no bones.

234
An Atlantic hagfish is a slimy, fish-like animal of the abyss with disgusting eating habits. It is nearly blind but has a good sense of smell, which helps it to find prey. A hagfish has tentacles and hooks around its mouth to grab hold of its victim's flesh. Then it burrows into the prey's body, eating its insides. A hagfish can survive for many months without feeding again.

235
The most common fish in the Abyssal Zone are called rattails, or grenadiers. There are around 300 different types of rattails in the world and scientists estimate that there are at least 20 billion of just one type – that's more than three times the number of humans!

▼ Rattails are slow movers so they probably creep up on their prey to catch them. They are also scavengers, eating anything they can find on the seabed. Here, they swarm around a bait cage and the submersible *Mir I*.

236 One of the world's strongest types of glass is made by a creature of the abyss. The Venus' flower basket is a type of glass sponge that has a strong skeleton. Glass sponges build their structures from strands of silica, the material used to make glass.

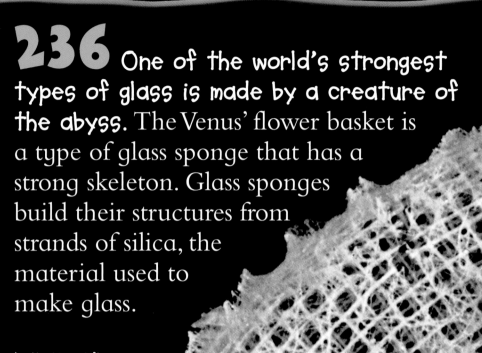

▶ The Venus' flower basket lives at depths of 5000 metres in the ocean waters of Southeast Asia.

237 Sponges are the simplest of all animals. Most sponges live in oceans and they are attached to solid surfaces. Since they can't move to find food, sponges create water currents that move through their bodies so they can filter out any particles of food.

Osculum

Flow of water

Spicules (strands of silica)

Pore

▶ Special cells near the pores have tail-like parts, that move in a beating motion. This sucks water into the sponge, and out through the osculum.

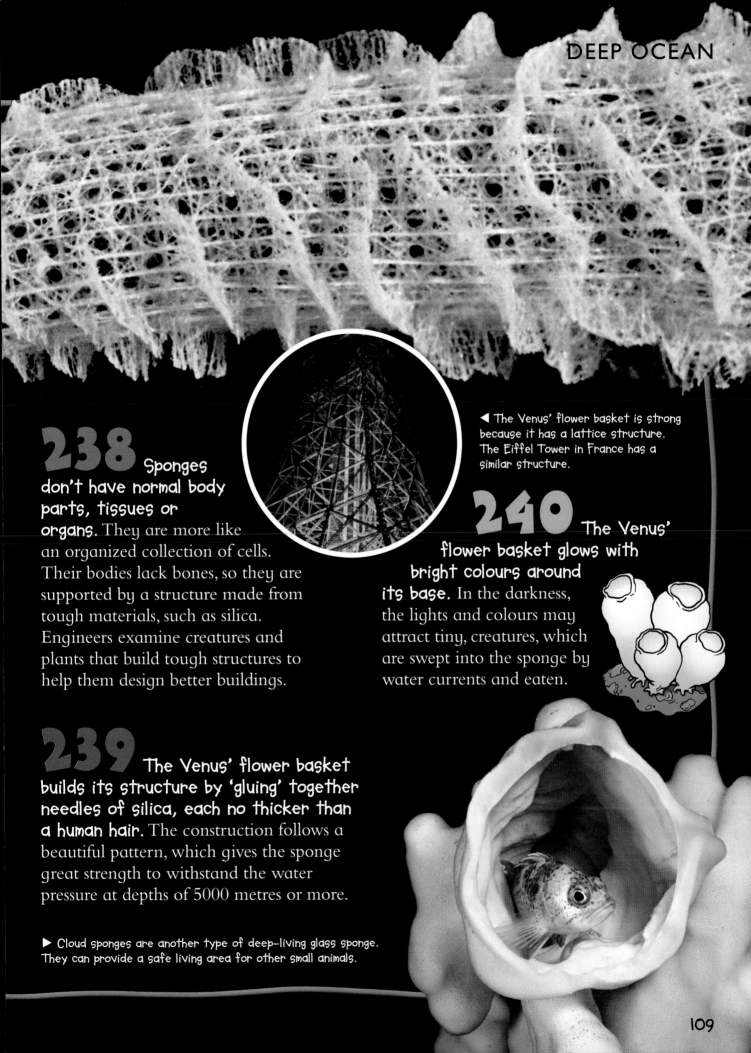

◀ The Venus' flower basket is strong because it has a lattice structure. The Eiffel Tower in France has a similar structure.

238 Sponges don't have normal body parts, tissues or organs. They are more like an organized collection of cells. Their bodies lack bones, so they are supported by a structure made from tough materials, such as silica. Engineers examine creatures and plants that build tough structures to help them design better buildings.

240 The Venus' flower basket glows with bright colours around its base. In the darkness, the lights and colours may attract tiny, creatures, which are swept into the sponge by water currents and eaten.

239 The Venus' flower basket builds its structure by 'gluing' together needles of silica, each no thicker than a human hair. The construction follows a beautiful pattern, which gives the sponge great strength to withstand the water pressure at depths of 5000 metres or more.

▶ Cloud sponges are another type of deep-living glass sponge. They can provide a safe living area for other small animals.

The Hadal Zone

241 The oceans plunge to depths greater than 6000 metres in only a few places, called trenches. This is called the Hadal Zone, named after the Greek word 'hades', which means 'unseen'. It's the perfect name for the most mysterious habitat on Earth.

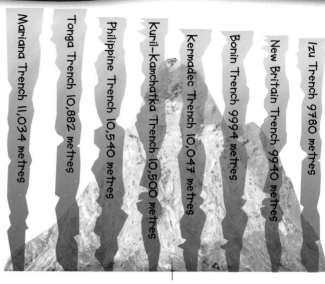

Mariana Trench 11,034 metres
Tonga Trench 10,882 metres
Philippine Trench 10,540 metres
Kuril-Kamchatka Trench 10,500 metres
Kermadec Trench 10,047 metres
Bonin Trench 9994 metres
New Britain Trench 9940 metres
Izu Trench 9780 metres

Mount Everest 8850 metres

▲ Earth's largest mountain, Everest, could fit into eight of the world's deepest trenches.

242 The deepest of all trenches is the Mariana Trench in the Pacific Ocean, which plunges to 11,034 metres. It is 2550 kilometres long and about 70 kilometres wide. This trench was created when two massive plates in the Earth's crust collided millions of years ago.

243 Scientists know very little about animals that live in the Hadal Zone. Collecting live animals from this depth causes great problems because their bodies are suited to high water pressure. When they are brought to the surface the pressure drops, and they die.

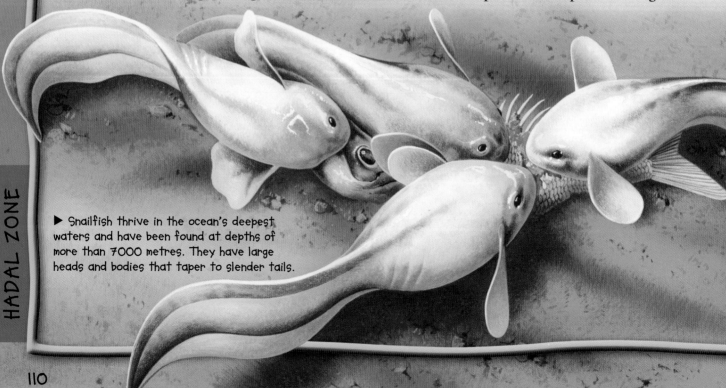

► Snailfish thrive in the ocean's deepest waters and have been found at depths of more than 7000 metres. They have large heads and bodies that taper to slender tails.

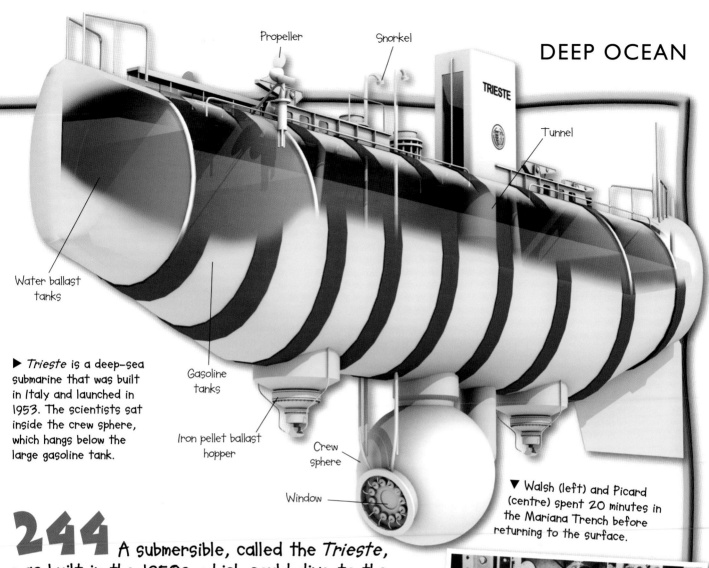

Propeller

Snorkel

TRIESTE

Tunnel

Water ballast tanks

► *Trieste* is a deep-sea submarine that was built in Italy and launched in 1953. The scientists sat inside the crew sphere, which hangs below the large gasoline tank.

Gasoline tanks

Iron pellet ballast hopper

Crew sphere

Window

▼ Walsh (left) and Picard (centre) spent 20 minutes in the Mariana Trench before returning to the surface.

244 A submersible, called the *Trieste*, was built in the 1950s, which could dive to the Hadal Zone. In 1960, explorers Don Walsh and Jacques Piccard climbed aboard and began one of the most dangerous journeys ever undertaken. It took five hours to descend to 10,911 metres in the Mariana Trench and here they saw the deepest-known crustacean – a red shrimp. Other similar creatures called amphipods have been collected at depths of 10,500 metres.

CURIOUS CREATURES

Draw a picture of your own Hadal Zone creature. It should probably be dark-coloured, with tiny eyes, or none at all, and very ugly. Body parts that help it feel its way around a dark habitat would be helpful.

245 The deepest-living fish are believed to belong to a family called *Abyssobrotula*. One fish, *Abyssobrotula galatheae*, was captured in 1970 at a depth of 8370 metres. It was found by explorers in the Puerto Rico Trench. Scientists tried to bring the fish to the surface, but it did not survive the journey.

Muds and oozes

246 The remains of all marine creatures eventually get eaten or drift down to the seabed. These remains, which are mostly marine snow, become deep-sea sediments. They form layers of muddy ooze that can be up to 450 metres thick.

247 Most creatures that live on the seabefare scavengers. A dead whale can provide food for millions of other animals, including shrimp-like amphipods and copepods, worms, rattails and hagfish.

Greenland shark

Amphipods

Rattails

Hagfish

KEY

① Crabs, hagfish, amphipods, rattails and sharks strip the flesh from the fresh body.

② Next, worms are the main colonizers, living off the enriched sediments.

③ Finally, the whale's bones produce sulphides — chemicals that bacteria, mussels and clams feast on.

248 The muddy layer of the abyssal plain may look smooth, but close up there are tiny trails and holes. Every handful of mud contains millions of microscopic animals. Foraminifera and radiolarians are tiny shelled single-celled organisms that live in the sediments. When they die, their shells dissolve into the muddy ooze.

249 The abyssal plains are home to many types of sea cucumbers. These sausage-shaped animals are common in this habitat. Some burrow in the mud, while others can swim. Most move over the seafloor, picking up any bits of food they can find.

▼ It can take up to 100 years for a whale carcass to be devoured. More than 30,000 different types of animal feed and live off the carcass at different stages.

Mussels and clams

③

Bacterial mat

②

Squat lobster

Polychaete worms

I DON'T BELIEVE IT!

The seabed of the Antarctic Ocean has some mega-sized animals. Scientists found giant spiders and worms, and fish with huge eyes and body parts that scientists described as 'dangly bits'!

250 Tripod fish have very long spines, called rays, on their fins. They use these to stand on the muddy seabed without sinking as they wait for prey to drift by. They are almost blind but can sense vibrations made by other animals nearby.

▼ Tripod fish stand still for hours at a time, facing the water currents, and wait for food to drift towards them.

Deep heat

251 **The deep ocean floor is mainly a cold place, where animals struggle to survive.** However, there are some extraordinary areas where the water is heated to temperatures of 400°C and living things thrive.

252 **Below the Earth's surface is a layer of hot, semi-liquid rock, called magma.** In places, magma is close to the ocean floor. Water seeps into cracks in rocks, called hydrothermal vents, and is heated. The water dissolves minerals from the rocks as it travels up towards the ocean floor, and bursts through a vent like a fountain.

253 **The first hydrothermal vents were discovered in the Pacific Ocean in the 1970s.** Since then, others have been found in the Atlantic, Indian and Arctic Oceans. The largest known region of hydrothermal vents lies near the Mid-Atlantic Ridge and is the size of a football pitch.

▼ The minerals in the water produce dark clouds that look like smoke, and these vents are called 'black smokers'. Over time, they build up rocky structures called chimneys, which can grow to the height of a 15-storey building.

KEY

1. Vent mussel
2. Ratfish
3. Vent crab
4. Vent octopus
5. Chimney
6. Sea spider
7. Tube worms

254 Some hydrothermal vents do not support much life, other than microscopic creatures. Others support colonies of limpets, shrimps, starfish and tube worms, which survive without any sunlight. They are able to live and grow due to the minerals in the super-heated water from the vents.

▲ Hydrothermal vents known as 'white smokers' release cooler water and plumes of different minerals to black smokers.

255 Vent tube worms can grow to 2 metres long and they live without eating anything. Each worm is attached to the seabed and is protected by the tube it lives in. A red plume at the top collects seawater, which is rich in minerals. These minerals are passed to bacteria in the worm's body, and are then turned into nutrients.

⑥

⑦

Plume

Blood vessel

Heart

Bacteria

Tube

◀ Bacteria that live inside the tube worm turn the minerals into food, which the worm needs to survive.

UNDER PRESSURE

You will need:
milk carton sticky tape

With an adult's help, make four holes on one side of an old milk carton, one above the other. Put sticky tape over the holes and fil the carton with water. Hold it over a bowl while you pull the tape off. Water will pour out fastest from the bottom hole because it has the most pressure on it.

Deep-sea coral

256 Tiny creatures called coral polyps build large reefs in the cold, deep ocean. Coral reefs are often found in warm, shallow waters, and they attract a wide variety of life. Cold-water reefs are less varied habitats, but there may be more cold-water reefs than warm-water ones.

257 Coral polyps have tube-shaped bodies and tentacles around their mouths. All polyps feed by filtering food particles from the water, and they have thousands of tiny stingers to stun bigger prey.

258 Coral polyps produce a hard substance called calcium carbonate, which forms a protective cup around them. Over time, the stony cups collect and grow into a reef, held together by a cement of sand, mud and other particles.

I DON'T BELIEVE IT!

Air pollution from carbon dioxide causes the oceans to become more acidic. This stops polyps, especially cold-water ones, from being able to grow their stony skeletons.

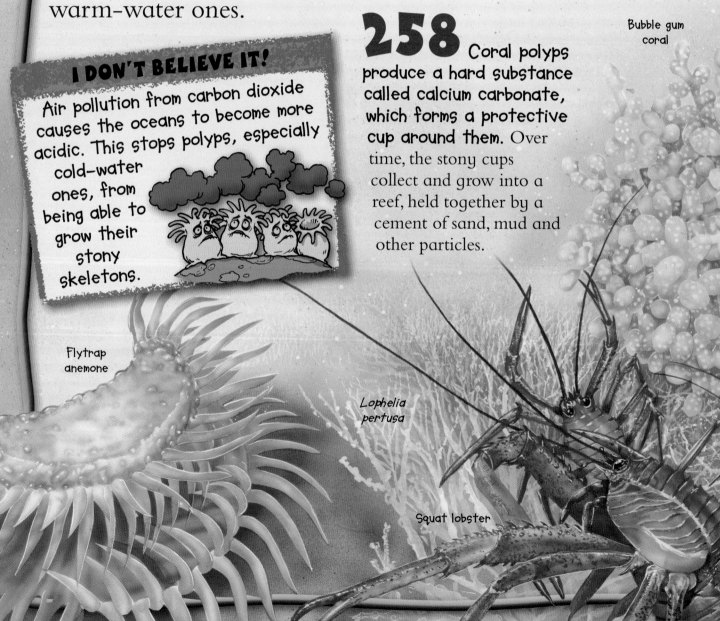

Bubble gum coral

Flytrap anemone

Lophelia pertusa

Squat lobster

▲ A specimen of bamboo coral is carefully lifted from the deep sea in a collection box that is attached to a submersible.

259
A type of cold-water coral polyp called *Lophelia* is the most common reef builder in the Atlantic Ocean. One reef can cover 2000 square kilometres and is home to animals such as squat lobsters, long-legged crabs, and fish – especially babies called larvae.

260
Other cold-water communities have been found in the deep oceans. Engineers drilling for oil in the Gulf of Mexico found cold seeps (places where gases leak out of cracks in the rocks) and animal life thrived nearby. The gases are an energy source for bacteria that feed there. Animals that feed on the bacteria are in turn eaten by crabs, corals, worms and fish.

▼ Cold-water coral creates a special habitat where other animals can live, find food and shelter. A group of living things that depend on one habitat like this is called an ecosystem.

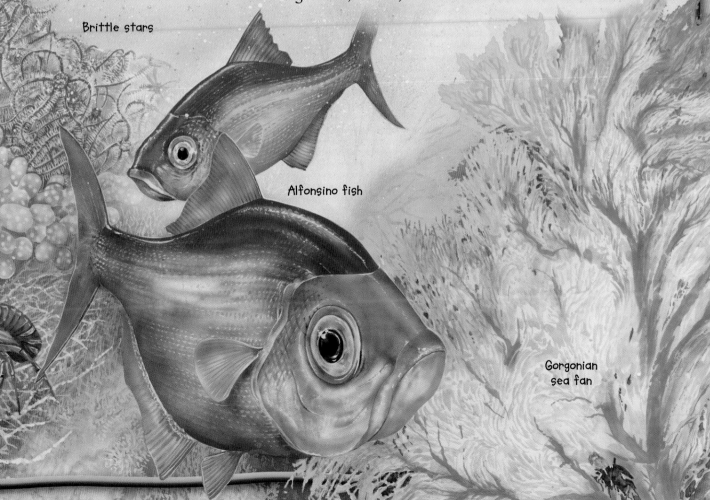

Brittle stars

Alfonsino fish

Gorgonian sea fan

On the move

261 Travelling in the ocean is different from travelling in air. Animals can simply float or drift along because they weigh 50 times less in water than they do in air. Currents help too. They can bring food to animals that are attached to the seabed, or they can carry animals towards food.

◄ Little sea butterflies are a type of sea snail. They can swim slowly through the water by flapping their 'wings', or they float in the currents.

▼ For this tube anemone, being attached to the seabed means it is impossible to make a quick getaway from the giant nudibranch that is attacking it (bottom).

262 Animals caught in deep-sea currents have to go with the flow, unless they are strong swimmers. Swimming takes 830 times as much energy as staying still because water is dense and heavy. Tiny zooplankton are weak swimmers, so when they get caught in currents, they drift along until they become free.

263 Many marine animals cannot move from one place to another. They are attached to the seabed and stay there, waiting for food to come to them. These animals, such as sea lilies and tube anemones, have feathery tentacles that they use to filter the seawater and collect particles of food.

264
Billions of animals undertake a journey every night. They travel up from the Twilight and Dark Zones into the Light Zone to feed, and return to deeper water in the morning. This mass movement is called a vertical migration and it represents the largest migration, or animal journey, on Earth.

265
Lantern fish are mighty movers of the ocean. The champion is called *Ceratoscopelus warmingii* and it lives at a depth of 1800 metres in the day. At night it swims upwards to depths of 100 metres to feed and avoid predators, and then it swims back. This feat is like a person running three marathons in a day!

DAY

Albatross

Phytoplankton

30 metres

Copepods

Comb jellies

Jellyfish

200 metres

Blue shark

Squid

Sperm whale

Lantern fish

1000 metres

NIGHT

Albatross

Mackerel

Phytoplankton

Comb jellies

Copepods

Lantern fish

Jellyfish

Squid

Blue shark

Sperm whale

◀▲ About half of all marine creatures move upwards at night towards the Light Zone where there is plenty of food. They descend to lower depths when the sun rises.

Breathing and diving

Gill slits

▲ As a shark swims, water enters its mouth, passes over its gills where oxygen is absorbed, and then leaves through the gill slits.

MAKE A SWIM BLADDER

Blow up a balloon. It is now filled with gas, like a swim bladder. Put the balloon in a bowl or bath of water and try to make it sink. Now fill the balloon with water, and see if it will float.

266 Animals need to take a gas called oxygen into their bodies to release energy from food. Taking in oxygen is called breathing, and the process of using it to release energy is respiration. Most marine animals are specially adapted to take in dissolved oxygen from seawater.

267 Fish breathe using gills. Like our lungs take oxygen from air, gills take in oxygen from water. Most fish also have a swim bladder, which helps them to cope with the changing pressure as they swim deeper. A swim bladder is a gas-filled sac that expands as a fish moves upwards, and shrinks as it descends. All deep-sea fish have gills, but they do not have swim bladders because the immense pressure would crush them.

Blowhole

◀ Whales, such as this killer whale, come to the surface to breathe. They have one or two blowholes on the top of their heads. These are like nostrils, and this is where air enters the body. When air is breathed out of a blowhole it creates a water spout.

As a sperm whale dives, its ribs and lungs contract (shrink). They expand again when the whale surfaces.

The whale's heartbeat slows by half so less oxygen is needed.

The spermaceti organ is a huge mass of oil. It probably helps the whale to dive deep by changing its ability to float.

The nasal passages fill with cool water to help the whale sink.

▲ The sperm whale is adapted for diving in very deep water. It can stay underwater for up to 90 minutes while hunting for giant squid.

268 Seals, dolphins and whales are air-breathing mammals, but their bodies are adapted to life in water. The sperm whale can store oxygen in its blood and muscles, which allows it to descend to over 1000 metres to hunt. Its flexible ribcage allows the whale's lungs to shrink during a dive.

269 Super-speedy pilot whales are called 'cheetahs of the deep'. During the day, these predators swim at depths of around 300 metres, but at night they plunge to 1000 metres in search of prey. Pilot whales can plummet 9 metres a second at top swimming speed. They need to be fast to catch their prey of large squid, but also because they need to get back to the surface to breathe.

▼ Most marine worms have feathery gills that absorb oxygen from the water. However, some do not have gills and absorb oxygen through their skin.

270 Simple creatures do not have special body parts for breathing. They can absorb oxygen from the water directly through their skins. The amount of oxygen in the water falls from the surface to a depth of around 1000 metres, but it increases again at greater depths.

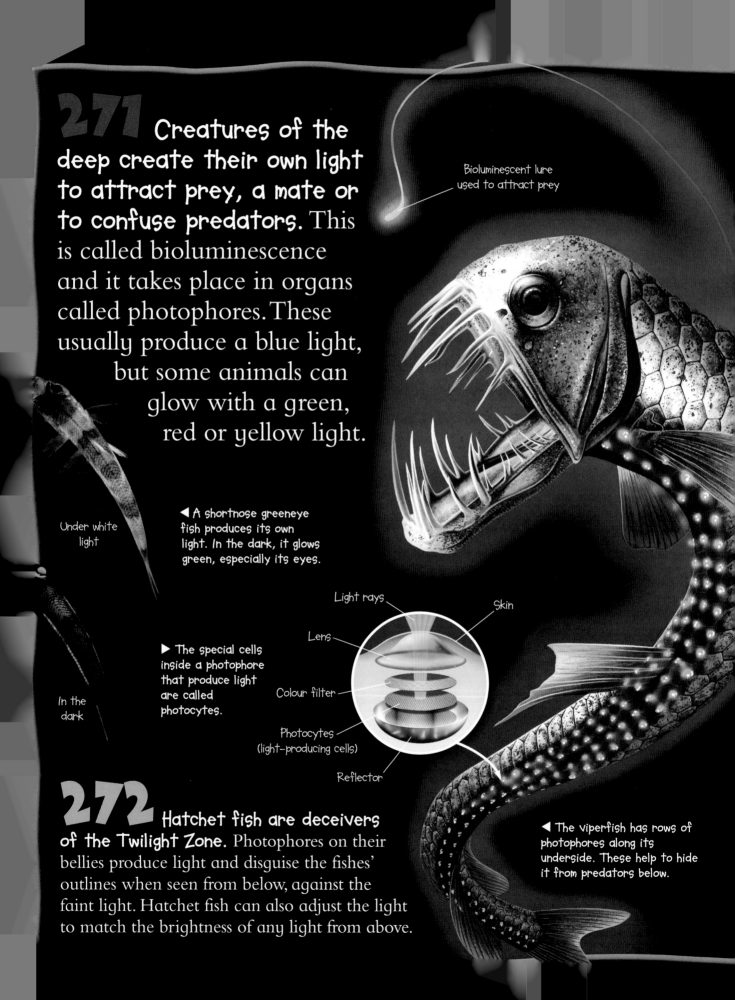

271 Creatures of the deep create their own light to attract prey, a mate or to confuse predators. This is called bioluminescence and it takes place in organs called photophores. These usually produce a blue light, but some animals can glow with a green, red or yellow light.

Bioluminescent lure used to attract prey

◀ A shortnose greeneye fish produces its own light. In the dark, it glows green, especially its eyes.

Under white light

In the dark

▶ The special cells inside a photophore that produce light are called photocytes.

Light rays

Lens

Skin

Colour filter

Photocytes (light-producing cells)

Reflector

272 Hatchet fish are deceivers of the Twilight Zone. Photophores on their bellies produce light and disguise the fishes' outlines when seen from below, against the faint light. Hatchet fish can also adjust the light to match the brightness of any light from above.

◀ The viperfish has rows of photophores along its underside. These help to hide it from predators below.

273 Spotted lantern fish use their photophores to attract mates. They are one of the brightest deep-sea fish, with brilliant displays of bioluminescence along their sides and bellies. The photophores are arranged in different patterns depending on whether the fish is male or female, and what type of lantern fish it is. This helps the fish to find the right mate.

274 It is not just fish that can glow in the dark. Mauve stinger jellyfish emit a beautiful violet-blue colour when they are disturbed. Firefly squid not only cover their bodies with lights, they can also produce a cloud of glowing particles that distracts predators while they make a quick getaway.

Mauve stinger jellyfish produce quick flashes of light when they sense movement in the water. They even flash when waves pass over them at the ocean's surface.

275 Tiny vampire squid have enormous eyes and can produce light all over their bodies whenever they want to. These squid are able to control their bioluminescence, producing dazzling displays of patterned light that can be dimmed or brightened, probably to scare off predators. When a vampire squid is hunting it does not light up. This means it can surprise its prey.

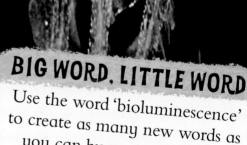

BIG WORD, LITTLE WORD
Use the word 'bioluminescence' to create as many new words as you can by rearranging the letters. Each word must be at least two letters long. Use a dictionary to check the spelling of your words.

Deep-sea food

276 **The ocean food chain begins in the Light Zone.** Phytoplankton use the Sun's energy to grow. In turn, they are eaten by other creatures, passing on energy and nutrients. It takes a long time for energy and nutrients to filter down to the sea floor, so many deep-sea animals scavenge food, eating whatever they find, while others hunt.

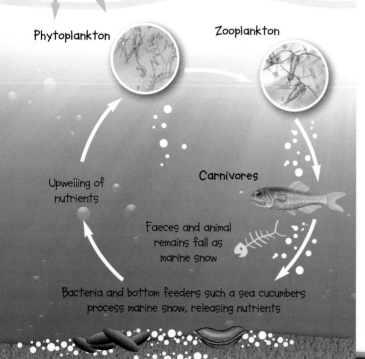

▼ Nearly all energy used by marine life comes from the Light Zone. Phytoplankton begin the nutrient cycle, and upward-flowing water currents complete it by bringing nutrients back to the surface.

Sun

Phytoplankton

Zooplankton

Carnivores

Upwelling of nutrients

Faeces and animal remains fall as marine snow

Bacteria and bottom feeders such a sea cucumbers process marine snow, releasing nutrients

277 **Copepods and krill (zooplankton) may be small but they play a big role in the deep-ocean ecosystem.** These tiny, plant-eating crustaceans exist in their billions. They swim up to the surface every evening to try to avoid being eaten. In the morning they swim back down into the deep, dark waters. Krill can live to depths of 2000 metres.

I DON'T BELIEVE IT!

One krill is not much bigger than a paperclip, but the total weight of all the krill in the world is greater than the total weight of all the people on the planet!

◄ Goblin sharks have soft, flabby bodies and long, strange-looking snouts. They are pinkish white in colour.

280 **Fangtooth fish are also known as ogrefish.** They use their unusually sharp, long teeth to grab hold of squid and fish. Food is scarce in the deep ocean, but with such large jaws, fangtooths attempt to eat almost any prey that comes along, even animals that are larger than themselves.

278 **Large predators, such as sharks, seals and whales, may reach the Dark Zone, but few go deeper.** Goblin sharks swim slowly in the Dark Zone and they have snouts that may help them to find food. Their huge jaws can snap forwards to grab prey such as small fish and squid.

▼ Gulper eels can grown to 2 metres in length. They have pink photophores on their tails to attract prey.

► This soft-bodied animal called a predatory tunicate lives in the Twlight Zone. When an animal swims into its hood-like mouth it closes shut like a Venus flytrap.

279 **Gulper eels are all mouth.** These predators of the Dark Zone have enormous mouths, but small teeth. It may be that gulper eels use their big mouths for catching lots of small prey at a time, rather than one large, meaty prey.

Anglerfish

281 If you cannot find food in the dark, make it come to you! Anglerfish have long growths on their heads that work like fishing rods, and the tips are coated in glowing bacteria. Other animals are attracted to the glowing light, called a lure, and are quickly snapped up by the anglerfish.

I DON'T BELIEVE IT!

Pacific blackdragons are dark on the outside, and the inside! Their stomachs are black so when they swallow fish that glow, the light doesn't show and encourage predators to approach!

▲ In the 2003 Disney Pixar movie *Finding Nemo*, Marlin and Dory narrowly escape the jaws of an anglerfish.

282 There are many different types of anglerfish and all look very strange. The hairy anglerfish is one of the strangest and it lives at depths of up to 1500 metres. It gets its name from its fins, which have long spikes, and the sensitive hairs that cover its body.

Tassel-chinned angler

Long-rod angler

Deep-sea angler

Males

▶ Two tiny males are attached to this female Regan's anglerfish. These anglerfish are sometimes called phantom anglerfish.

283 Finding a mate in the dark can be tough, so some male anglerfish stay attached to a female! The males are much smaller than the females, so they can grab hold and hitch a lift that lasts for life. While scientists have found many types of female anglerfish they are still searching for some of their tiny male relations!

285 A dragonfish also lures prey to its death. When a dragonfish spies a shrimp to eat it produces a red spotlight made by photophores below its eyes. The shrimp can't see red, so it is unaware it is being hunted. The dragonfish then snaps up its prey in its large mouth, full of ultra-sharp teeth.

▼ Monkfish are so well camouflaged that they are almost impossible to spot when lying on the ocean floor.

284 Anglers are types of anglerfish that lie on the seafloor. Their wide, flat bodies are covered in soft, fleshy growths that help them to blend in with the mud where they hide. Anglers use their fins to shuffle along, flicking their lures as they go. They are often caught and sold as food, and also better known as monkfish.

Hide and seek

286 Many animals use colours and patterns to hide from predators or prey. In the deep oceans, colours appear different because of the way light is absorbed by water. Colours, other than black and red, are not very useful for camouflage. Deep-sea creatures have developed special ways to avoid being detected.

▲ Deep-sea glass squid are mostly transparent, apart from some brightly coloured polka dots on their bodies.

287 Some deep-sea animals are well adapted for hiding and seeking. Glass squid are almost completely transparent, so light passes through their bodies, helping them go unnoticed. A thin body can help too, because it is hard to see from certain angles. With little light around, enormous eyes are useful. Big eyes can collect more light and turn it into hazy images.

▲ Spookfish have enormous eyes, giving them very good vision.

288 Silvery scales on a fish's back are perfect for reflecting light and confusing a predator. When shimmering scales are seen against dim rays of light in the Twilight Zone, the outline of a fish's body becomes less obvious, and it fades into the background or even disappears.

Silvery, reflective scales

Light-producing photophores

▲ By using their photophores to produce light and their silvery scales to reflect light, hatchet fish become almost invisible to predators.

289 In the dark, animals rely on senses other than sight. Many deep-sea animals can feel vibrations in the water. Shrimp have sensory organs all over their bodies, including their antennae, which can detect movements nearby. Many fish can also sense the small electrical fields generated by other living things.

▶ The snipe eel's jaws curve away from each other so they never fully close.

290 Snipe eels have long, ribbon-like bodies, and jaws that look like a bird's bill. They live at depths of up to 1800 metres and can grown to 1.5 metres in length. As males mature their jaws shrink, but their nostrils grow longer. This probably improves their sense of smell and helps them to find females.

QUIZ

Which of these animals uses colour and pattern to scare other animals, rather than to hide?

Zebra   Wasp   Tiger
Leaf insect
Arctic fox

Answer:
Wasp

Searching the deep

▼ This timeline shows how technology has developed, improving ways of exploring the deep ocean.

291 Early ocean explorers had to overcome many problems. Divers needed a supply of air and to be able to cope with the water pressure. If divers ascend too quickly, the sudden change in pressure can cause the bends – a life-threatening sickness.

1775 The *Turtle* was an early, one-man submarine

1837 The waterproof Siebe diving suit was developed

1872 HMS *Challenger* set sail for a four-year study of the deep ocean

1882 The USS *Albatross* continued this important research

1925 *Meteor* began mapping the seafloor

292 The first diving suit was invented in the 1830s. It was made of waterproof canvas and rubber, and allowed divers to descend to around 60 metres. About 40 years later a ship called the HMS *Challenger* explored the deeper oceans.

Thruster   Oxygen supply   Boat cable

1934 William Beebe and Otis Barton used a bathysphere to make the first deep-ocean dive

293 Today's deep-diving suits are made of metal. These Newt Suits allow divers to work at a depth of 300 metres. Suits have thrusters to help divers move underwater, communication systems to link to the boat at the surface, and video cameras.

▲ Newt Suits have joints, so divers can move their arms and legs.

Pincer

294 *Alvin* was the first submersible that could take explorers deep into the Dark Zone.
It has made more than 4500 dives, and it was on one of these that hydrothermal vents were first discovered. A programme of modernization means *Alvin* will be able to reach depths exceeding 6000 metres.

296 There are other ways to find out the secrets of the deep, including taking pictures from space.
Satellite images provide information about deep water currents and the undersea landscape. Sonar is a method that maps the ocean floor by bouncing sound signals off the seabed.

1960 *Trieste* dived to the Mariana Trench

1964 Deep-sea submarine *Alvin* was built

1984 The *Nautile* can carry up to three people to depths of 6000 metres

1987 The Newt Suit was developed

1990s Satellites were used to map the seafloor

1988 *Jason*, an underwater ROV, was launched

295 One of the safest ways to explore the deep is using a Remotely Operated Vehicle, or ROV.
These unmanned submersibles are lowered to the seabed by cables and are operated by the crew of a ship on the surface. In future, ROVs will be able to operate without cables, so they will be able to move around more freely.

▶ The Monterey Bay Aquarium Research Institute has developed a deep-sea robot called the Benthic Rover. It is helping scientists discover more about the effects of global warming on the oceans.

KEY
1 Video camera
2 Water current meter
3 Respirometer measures gases in the sediments

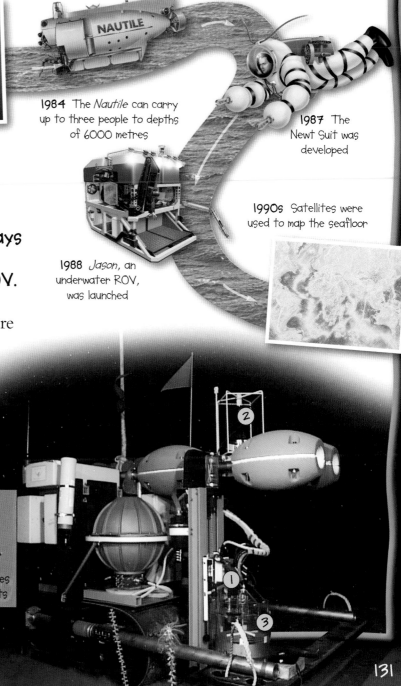

Sea changes

297 Billions of years ago, life began in the oceans – and this environment is still home to most living things. Every part of the ocean matters, from the shallow seashores to the deepest trenches. It not only provides habitats for marine animals and plants, it also provides us with food and greatly affects our atmosphere and climate.

▶ Robot submersibles are used to gather valuable information about the deep ocean. They can deploy bait cages to attract animals for observation and research, and collect samples to take back to the surface for further study.

298 Overfishing threatens all sea life. Krill, for example, are an important source of energy for billions of ocean creatures, but they are now being harvested in huge amounts, especially in the Antarctic. There is a danger that if too much krill is taken for humans to eat, there will not be enough left to support the ocean ecosystems, including deep-ocean life.

299 Pollution is a major problem — rubbish is dumped in the oceans, tankers leak oil and the crisis of carbon dioxide pollution looms. This is caused by burning fossil fuels, which pollutes ocean water and causes the climate to heat up. A new plan is to use the deep oceans to store carbon dioxide. This gas would be collected from power stations and buried deep in the seabed, in a process called carbon capture and storage.

300 The precious deep-ocean habitat is being destroyed by humans faster than we can uncover its mysteries. However in recent times, people have begun to understand how important it is to respect the oceans and protect their wildlife. Hopefully there is time for nations to work together to avoid further damage, and uncover new secrets of the deep.

I DON'T BELIEVE IT!

If you could take all living things on Earth and fill a giant box with them, ocean life would take up 99.5% of it. The leftover space could hold everything that lives on land!

WHALES AND DOLPHINS

301 Whales, dolphins and porpoises are a fascinating group of marine animals also known as cetaceans. Like other members of the mammal animal group, they have warm blood and breathe air. Almost all kinds live in the sea, apart from a few species of dolphin that live in freshwater rivers and lakes. This intelligent group holds many records – the biggest animal in the world, the largest hunter, and some of the fastest, deepest-diving creatures ever to have lived.

▶ Many kinds of dolphin live in groups called schools. Common dolphins are colourful, with yellow or tan patches along their sides and dark 'spectacles' around their eyes.

The greatest animals

302 Whales are the biggest kind of animal alive today. Some are longer and heavier than the largest trucks. They need lots of muscle power and energy to move such large bodies. As they live in the ocean, the water helps to support their huge bulk.

303 The blue whale is the largest animal ever. It can grow up to 30 metres in length, which is as long as seven cars placed end to end. It reaches up to 150 tonnes in weight – that's as heavy as 35 elephants.

▶ The blue whale is a true giant, as large as a submarine. Yet it is also gentle and swims slowly, unless frightened or injured.

304
On land, bears and tigers are the biggest hunting animals. However, the sperm whale is more than 100 times larger, making it the biggest predator (active hunter) on Earth. It grows up to 20 metres in length and 50 tonnes in weight.

TRUE OR FALSE?

1. The sperm whale is the biggest predator.
2. The blue whale weighs up to 30 tonnes in weight.
3. Whales breathe oxygen through gills.

Answers:
1. True 2. False, it can weigh up to 150 tonnes 3. False

305
The animal with the largest mouth is the bowhead whale. Its body is 18 metres long, and its mouth makes up almost one-third of its length. Fin whales are the second largest whales, at an impressive 26 metres long.

▼ Killer whales come to the surface and open their nostrils, called blowholes, to breathe. They then dive back into the water again. The blowholes stay closed underwater.

306
Whales breathe air, just like humans. They must hold their breath as they dive underwater to feed. A few of them, such as the bottlenose whale, can stay underwater for more than one hour. Most humans have trouble holding their breath for even one minute!

▶ Bottlenose dolphins swim underwater for long periods of time, searching for food. They must then return to the surface to take in oxygen.

One big family

307 The mammal group of cetaceans is made up of about 80 kinds of whale, dolphin and porpoise. The whale group is then divided into two main types – baleen whales and toothed whales.

MAKE A DOLPHIN!

You will need:
paper   coloured pens or pencils
Draw a dolphin outline and colour it any pattern you like. You can name it after its colour, such as the pink-spotted dolphin. Or use your own name, like Claire's dolphin.

▼ The sperm whale is the biggest of the toothed whales. It only seems to have teeth in its lower jaw because those in its upper jaw can barely be seen.

308 Baleen whales are the largest members of the cetacean group. They are often called great whales. The sei whale, for example, is about 16 metres long. Baleen whales catch food with long strips in their mouths called baleen, or whalebone.

309 Toothed whales catch prey with their sharp teeth. This subgroup includes sperm whales, beaked whales and pilot whales. One example is the beluga, or white whale. It is one of the noisiest whales, making clicks, squeaks and trills.

◀ The beluga lives in the cold waters of the Arctic and can grow up to 5 metres in length.

138

▼ The finless porpoise, with its blunt 'beak' and bulging forehead, is one of the smallest cetaceans at about 1.5 metres in length.

310 Another group is made up of beaked whales. These are medium-sized whales with long, beak-shaped mouths. There are about 20 kinds, but some are very rare and hardly ever seen. The shepherd's beaked whale, which is about 7 metres in length, has been seen fewer than 20 times.

311 There are six species of porpoise. They are usually quite small, at 2 metres or less in length. They have blunter, more rounded heads than dolphins. The finless porpoise, as its name suggests, has a smooth back with no fin.

Grey patch from eye to the flipper

Back is a dusky blue-black colour

▶ The dusky dolphin is very inquisitive and likes to swim and leap near boats, perhaps in the hope of being fed.

White underside

312 There are more than 35 kinds of dolphin. Most of them are 2 to 3 metres in length. They are fast swimmers and can often be seen leaping above the waves. The dusky dolphin is one of the highest leapers, twisting and somersaulting before it splashes back into the sea.

Inside whales and dolphins

313 Whales, dolphins and porpoises are mammals. They have the same parts inside their bodies as humans. These include bones to make up the skeleton, lots of muscles, a stomach to hold food, a heart to pump blood, and lungs to breathe air.

314 Most mammals have hair or fur. Whales, dolphins and porpoises are unusual because they have smooth, hairless skin to make them streamlined. Only a few hairs, mainly bristles, can be found around the eyes, nose and mouth.

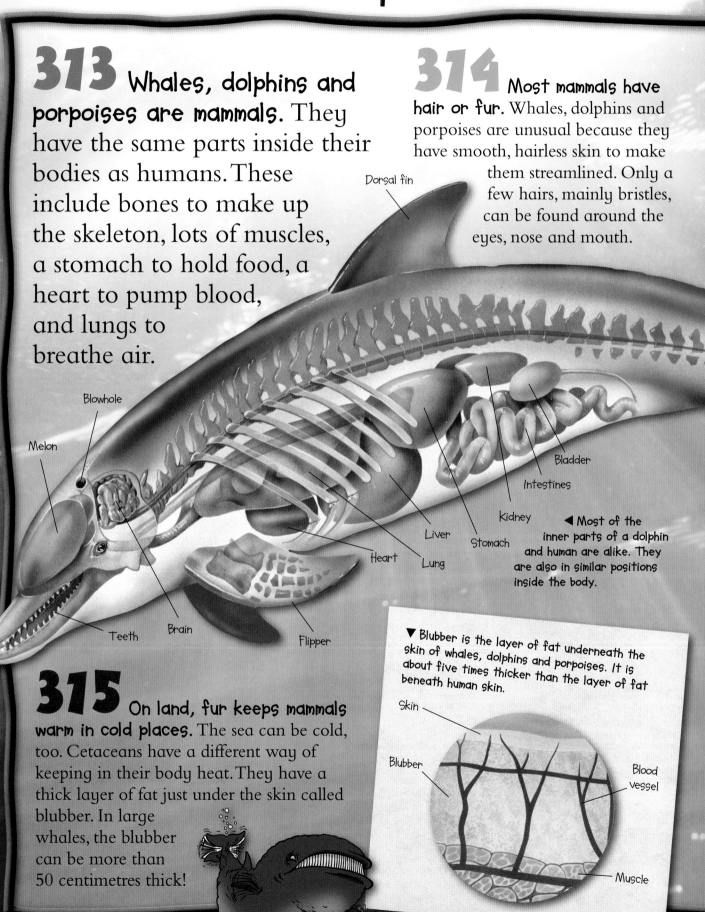

Dorsal fin

Blowhole

Melon

Bladder

Intestines

Kidney

Liver

Stomach

Heart

Lung

Teeth

Brain

Flipper

◄ Most of the inner parts of a dolphin and human are alike. They are also in similar positions inside the body.

▼ Blubber is the layer of fat underneath the skin of whales, dolphins and porpoises. It is about five times thicker than the layer of fat beneath human skin.

Skin

Blubber

Blood vessel

Muscle

315 On land, fur keeps mammals warm in cold places. The sea can be cold, too. Cetaceans have a different way of keeping in their body heat. They have a thick layer of fat just under the skin called blubber. In large whales, the blubber can be more than 50 centimetres thick!

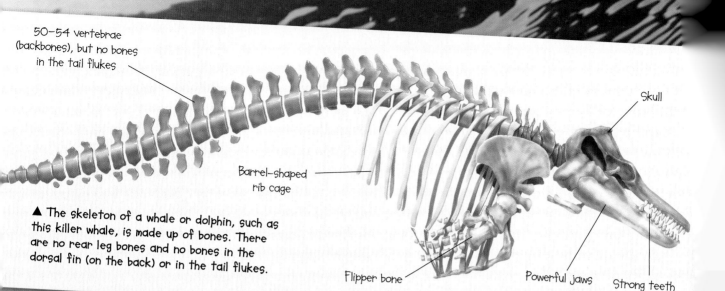

50–54 vertebrae (backbones), but no bones in the tail flukes

Skull

Barrel-shaped rib cage

Flipper bone

Powerful jaws

Strong teeth

▲ The skeleton of a whale or dolphin, such as this killer whale, is made up of bones. There are no rear leg bones and no bones in the dorsal fin (on the back) or in the tail flukes.

Fluke

316 Compared to most animals, whales, dolphins and porpoises have large brains for their size. Dolphins are clever creatures, able to learn tricks and solve simple puzzles. Some scientists believe that dolphins have even developed their own way of communicating.

317 Cetaceans often have small animals growing inside their bodies called parasites, such as lice. Parasites aren't needed for survival – the whale or dolphin provides them with food. Some baleen whales have their heads covered with barnacles (shellfish), which normally grow on seaside rocks.

I DON'T BELIEVE IT!

The sperm whale has the biggest brain in the world. It weighs about 8 kilograms – that's over five times the size of a human brain.
~~...its large brain does not mean~~

▲ Barnacles are a type of shellfish. They stick firmly to large whales and cannot be rubbed off!

Flippers, flukes and fins

318 Most mammals have four legs and a tail. Instead, whales, dolphins and porpoises have flippers, a fin and a tail. Flippers are their front limbs, similar to human arms. In fact, flipper bones and human arm and hand bones are alike. Flippers are mainly used for swimming, scratching and waving to send messages to others in the group.

319 The tail of a cetacean is in two almost identical parts. Each part is called a fluke. Unlike the flippers, flukes have no bones. They are used for swimming as the body arches powerfully to swish them up and down. They can also be slapped onto the water's surface to send messages to other whales. This is called lobtailing.

▼ Whales can often be seen splashing backwards into the water. This is known as breaching. Even the huge humpback whale can breach – and it weighs more than 30 tonnes!

Flipper-slapping
Humpbacks wave their flippers in the air and splash them onto the surface

Lobtailing
When the tail is slapped onto the water's surface

MAKE A WHALE!

You will need:

long balloon   newspaper strips
paints   papier-mâché paste

Paste three layers of newspaper onto the balloon. Let it dry, then paint the whale and stick on paper fins and a tail.

320 Many whales, dolphins and porpoises jump out of the water. They then crash back down again with a big splash – this is called breaching. It may be done to send a loud message to others in the group, or to try and get rid of skin pests, such as barnacles and whale lice.

321 The fin on the back of many whales, dolphins and porpoises is known as a dorsal fin. In some, such as the killer whale, it is tall and narrow. In others, such as the bottlenose dolphin, it is shaped like a swept-back triangle. Blue whales have a tiny dorsal fin near the tail. Right whales, bowheads, belugas and narwhals have no dorsal fin at all.

Blue whale

Killer whale

Bottlenose dolphin

▲ Many whales, dolphins and porpoises can be recognized by their distinctive dorsal fin shapes.

Sensitive senses

Whales, dolphins and porpoises have many of the same senses as humans. Like us, they use sight and hearing, but because they live underwater these senses detect very different surroundings. A whale's eyes have adapted to cope with underwater conditions far better than a human's.

▼ Atlantic spotted dolphins roll over and rub each other. It's like saying, "Hello, we're in the same school."

323 One sense that humans don't have, but whales, dolphins and porpoises do is the ability to detect magnetism. Some whales may 'feel' the Earth's weak magnetic force, which humans would detect using a compass. This magnetic sense may help them to find their way on their long journeys, or migrations, through the wide and featureless ocean.

324 Whales, dolphins and porpoises have very sensitive skin, so the sense of touch is important to them. They rub and stroke others in their group, or a partner during breeding time. A mother whale often caresses her baby to provide comfort and warmth.

QUIZ!

1. Do dolphins have a strong sense of taste?
2. Cetaceans use what word beginning with 'e' to sense objects?
3. Which sense do some whales use when migrating?

Answers:
1. No, it is very weak
2. Echolocation 3. Magnetic sense

325 Dolphins have a weak sense of smell, if any at all. Instead, they use their strong sense of taste to tell them about the foods they are eating. They can also taste the water. This lets them know what other bits of food might be drifting nearby.

326 Hearing is vital for whales, dolphins and porpoises. They don't have outer ears, like us. Instead, sounds in the water are detected inside the head. Many toothed whales find their way in dark water by making clicking sounds, then listening to the echoes that bounce off nearby objects. This method is called echolocation.

▶ Killer whales spyhop – look across the surface of the water – for the fins of others in their group or for signs of enemies, such as sharks.

Breathing and diving

327 Whales, dolphins and porpoises breathe air in and out of their lungs. They don't have gills to breathe underwater, like a fish, so they must hold their breath when diving. Air goes in and out of the body through the blowhole – a small opening on top of the head, just in front of the eyes. It works in a similar way to our nostrils.

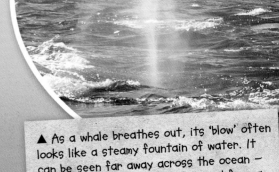

▲ As a whale breathes out, its 'blow' often looks like a steamy fountain of water. It can be seen far away across the ocean – and on a calm day, it can be heard from a distance, too.

▶ A giant squid tries to escape a sperm whale. The largest giant squid ever caught by a sperm whale was 12 metres in length.

328 When a whale comes to the surface after a dive, it breathes out air hard and fast. The moist air, mixed with slimy mucus from the whale's breathing passages, turns into water droplets. This makes the whale's breath look like a jet of steam or a fountain. It's called the 'blow'. All whales have 'blows' of different size and shape. This can help to identify them when they are hidden underwater.

329 Many cetaceans feed near the surface, so do not need to dive more than 50 metres down. The champion diver is the sperm whale. It can go down more than 3000 metres to hunt its prey of giant squid.

① The sperm whale surfaces and breathes in and out powerfully several times

② It then straightens out its body and may disappear beneath the surface

③ The whale then reappears and begins to arch its back

④ By arching its back and tipping its head downwards, the whale prepares to dive

⑤ Its tail is lifted out of the water as it begins to dive

⑥ The sperm whale dives deep into the darkness of the ocean

▶ The sperm whale is one of the greatest diving whales and may perform this sequence each time it dives to the cold, dark depths of the ocean.

330 Most dolphins and porpoises dive and hold their breath for one or two minutes. Large whales can stay underwater for a longer period of time, perhaps for 15 to 20 minutes. The sperm whale can dive for more than two hours!

Fierce hunters

331 **Dolphins, porpoises and toothed whales are active hunting carnivores.** They eat meat – the flesh of sea creatures, especially fish and squid. Some of them crunch up hard-shelled crabs, shrimps and prawns, or shellfish, such as oysters and whelks.

332 **Beaked whales mainly eat squid.** In some species, males have just two or four teeth, which look like tusks. Females have none at all. These whales suck in their prey and swallow it whole.

333 **A typical dolphin has 60 to 100 teeth.** They are in pairs, left and right, in the upper and lower jaws. These teeth are not usually thin and sharp like fangs, but wide and cone-shaped. The teeth are the same shape all along the jaw, unlike the teeth of a cat, dog or human. This is the best design for catching their slippery food.

▲ Dolphins swim around small fish that gather into a tight group called a 'bait-ball'. Then the dolphins dash into the bait-ball and try to grab the fish. From above shearwater seabirds divebomb the bait-ball as well.

▶ This bottlenose dolphin has found a tasty octopus to eat.

334 **Most dolphins and porpoises chase their speedy prey.** They quickly twist and turn in the water, snapping at victims. Once a dolphin catches its prey, it flicks it back into its mouth and swallows it whole. With a larger victim, the dolphin bites off a big chunk and swallows it. Whales, dolphins and porpoises hardly ever chew their food.

335 The sperm whale has about 50 teeth in its lower jaw, which are about 20 centimetres in length. The teeth in its upper jaw are so tiny, they can barely be seen.

Sieving the sea

336 Great whales are also called baleen whales because of the baleen in their mouths. Baleen is sometimes called whalebone, but it is not bone. It's light, tough and springy, like plastic. It hangs down in long strips from the whale's upper jaw. Baleen varies in size depending on the whale species.

▲ The bowhead whale's baleen hangs like a huge curtain, big enough for ten people to hide behind.

337 Most baleen whales, such as the blue, fin and sei, cruise-feed. This means that they feed by swimming slowly through a swarm of shrimp-like creatures called krill with their mouths open.

338 As a baleen whale feeds, it takes in a huge mouthful of water — enough to fill more than 100 bathtubs! This makes the skin around its throat expand like a balloon. The whale's food, such as krill, is in the water. The whale pushes the water out between the baleen plates. The baleen's bristles catch the krill like a giant filter. Then the whale licks off the krill and swallows them.

Baleen

339

The humpback whale makes a 'bubble curtain' to catch krill. It dives down, then swims up slowly in small circles as it breathes out. The bubbles created rise quickly and form a tube-shaped curtain that keeps the krill, or other food, close together in a bait-ball. The the humpback moves in to feed with its mouth open wide.

▲ When grey whales scoop up food from the seabed they can leave deep grooves like a ploughed field.

340

The grey whale often feeds on the shallow seabed. It swims on one side and drags its mouth through the mud. Then it pushes the water and mud out of its mouth. This traps food in its baleen, such as shellfish and shrimps.

◀ Humpback whales feed by rising up through shoals of fish with their mouths open and throat skin bulging. They scoop up water, push it out through the baleen and eat the food left inside their mouths.

I DON'T BELIEVE IT!

In summer, the blue whale eats 4 tonnes of food in one day! That's about four million krill. In winter, it eats hardly anything for many weeks because food is scarce.

Clicks, squeaks and squeals

341 Whales, dolphins and porpoises can be very noisy animals. They make loud clicks and whistles to help them navigate, hunt prey and communicate with each other. These noises travel long distances underwater, so divers can often hear them. Some whale noises can be head more than 100 kilometres away.

342 Sounds are especially important for detecting objects by echolocation. The dolphin detects the returning echoes of its own clicks. It can then work out the size and shape of objects nearby – whether a rock, coral, a shipwreck or a shoal of fish.

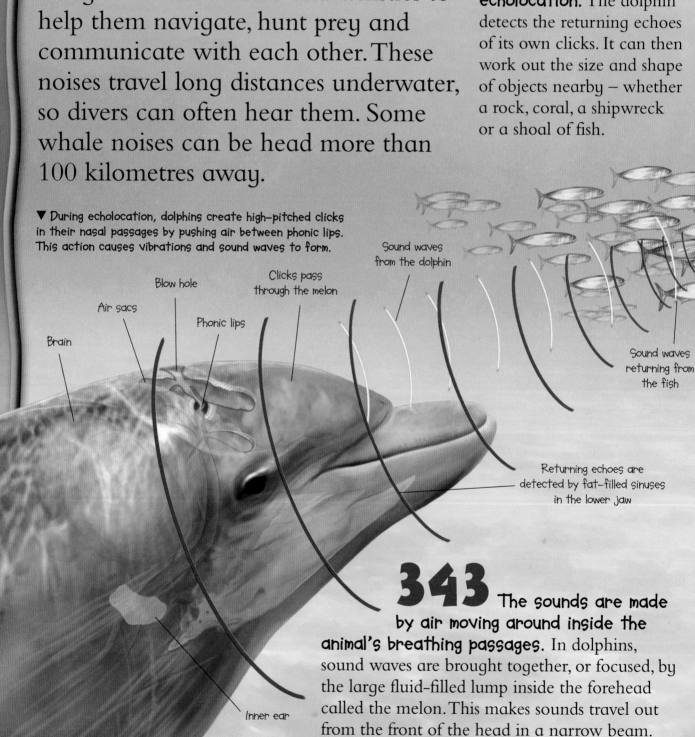

▼ During echolocation, dolphins create high-pitched clicks in their nasal passages by pushing air between phonic lips. This action causes vibrations and sound waves to form.

Brain

Air sacs

Blow hole

Phonic lips

Clicks pass through the melon

Sound waves from the dolphin

Sound waves returning from the fish

Returning echoes are detected by fat-filled sinuses in the lower jaw

Inner ear

343 The sounds are made by air moving around inside the animal's breathing passages. In dolphins, sound waves are brought together, or focused, by the large fluid-filled lump inside the forehead called the melon. This makes sounds travel out from the front of the head in a narrow beam.

344 Sounds are also used for communication. Belugas and dolphins especially make a vast range of clicks, squeals and squeaks. Sounds help them to stay together in their groups, and to work together when hunting fish.

◀ Scientists think that dolphins may use sound to identify other members of their pod.

◀ This whale is about to slap the surface of the water with its fluke. This is one way whales make noises with their bodies to talk to each other.

345 Scientists have spent time closely watching dolphins to see if they use a language to communicate. Certain sounds seem to occur more often when dolphins are resting, swimming, playing, feeding or breeding.

MAKE DOLPHIN NOISES
You will need:
sheet of card   ruler   plastic comb
Roll the card into a funnel and squeal through the narrow end. Rub the teeth of the comb along a ruler to produce dolphin-like clicks.

Long-distance swimmers

▶ Baleen whales, such as the humpback, travel long journeys so that they can give birth in tropical waters. Then the baby is able to grow stronger in calm waters before migrating to colder areas.

346 Many cetaceans migrate (go on long journeys) to find food at the same time each year. Baleen whales spend summer in cold northern or southern waters where there are vast amounts of food. For winter they swim back to the tropics. Although there is little food there, the water is warm and calm.

347 Baleen whales usually swim in groups as they migrate. They can often be seen 'spyhopping'. This means they swing around into an upright position, lift their heads above the water and turn slowly to look all around as they sink back into the water. This is especially common in whales that migrate along coasts.

I DON'T BELIEVE IT!

The migration of the grey whale takes less than six weeks. It would take a strong swimmer 30 weeks to complete the same journey.

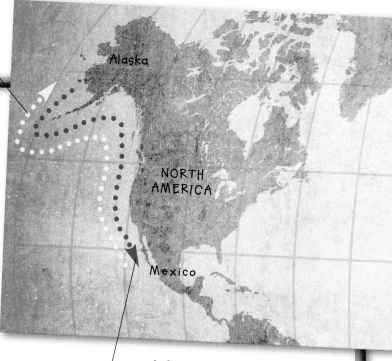

In summer, grey whales swim back to the coast of Alaska to feed

Alaska

NORTH AMERICA

Mexico

In winter, the whales travel south to Mexico to have babies

▲ Grey whales travel up to 20,000 kilometres every year, between the icy Arctic region and warm subtropical waters.

348 The grey whale makes the longest migration of any whale – and mammal. In spring, grey whales swim from their breeding areas in the subtropical waters around the coast of Mexico. They head north along the west coast of North America to the Arctic Ocean for summer feeding. In autumn, they return in the opposite direction.

349 Belugas and narwhals migrate from the cold waters of the southern area of the Arctic Ocean to the even icier waters further north! They follow the edge of the ice sheet as it shrinks and melts back each spring, then grows again each autumn.

◄ This conservation worker is fitting a satellite transmitter to a Beluga whale to keep track of its movements as it migrates.

350 Many cetaceans can now be tracked by satellite. A radio beacon is fixed, usually to the dorsal fin, and its signals are picked up by satellites in space. This shows that some whales complete exactly the same migration every year, while others wander far more widely around the oceans.

Family of Killers

351 All cetaceans are carnivores because they eat various kinds of animal as food. The killer whale can kill and eat almost any creature in the sea, from a small fish to a large whale. It is also known as the orca. It is not actually a whale, but the biggest member of the dolphin family.

352 Killer whales live in oceans all over the world. Their black-and-white markings make them easy to recognize. Males grow up to 9 metres in length and 10 tonnes in weight. They have tall, slim, triangular fins up to 2 metres in height. Females are slightly smaller and have lower, more rounded fins.

▼ A killer whale suddenly appears out of the surf and tries to grab an unsuspecting sea lion before it has time to escape.

▲ Cruising killer whales are constantly on the look for food. They listen and feel for splashes which may indicate nearby prey.

353 Killer whales live in groups called pods. A pod is like a big family. Normally, there are 20 to 30 whales in a pod. Older females are usually in charge. Throughout the year, the females decide where to travel, where to rest and when the pod will hunt.

354 Members of a killer whale pod communicate by making noises, such as clicks and grunts. They work together to surround a shoal of fish, such as tuna. The killer whale also feeds by 'surfing' onto a beach and grabbing a young seal or sea lion. Then the whale wriggles back into the sea, holding its victim by its sharp, back-curved teeth.

MAKE AN ORCA POD!

You will need:
white card   scissors   sticky tape
black pen   cotton thread

Draw and cut out killer whales of different sizes. Thread cotton through a small hole in the fin of all but the biggest whale. Then, dangle each whale from the larger whale by taping them to its body.

Fast and sleek

355 Dolphins are fast, active swimmers. They always seem to be looking for things to do, food to eat and friends to play with. They range in size from Commerson's dolphins, which are only 2 metres in length, to bottlenose dolphins, which are double the size at about 4 metres in length.

357 Spinner dolphins are well known for their spectacular leaps high into the air. Many dolphins somersault as they leap, but spinners twist and spin around as well, five or more times in each leap. They don't seem to mind if they land on their side, tail or head, and leap out to do it again.

356 Many dolphins like to bow-ride. This means riding in the bow wave of a ship or boat – the v-shaped wave made by the boat's sharp front end slicing through the water. Exactly why they do this is not clear. They may be waiting for leftover food to be thrown from the boat.

▶ This playful bottlenose dolphin is bow-riding. It may be saving energy by 'surfing' in the ship's wave.

I DON'T BELIEVE IT!

The long tusk-like tooth of the narwhal was once sold as the 'real horn' of the mythical horse, the unicorn.

▲ Dolphins are highly social animals that often live in large groups. This school of dolphins is are swimming, leaping and diving through the waves.

358 Dolphins are often seen swimming in large groups.
Several kinds of dolphin sometimes form even bigger groups of many thousands. Pantropical spotted dolphins form huge groups and are very active – leaping and swimming. From a distance, the sea can look like it is boiling!

359 Striped dolphins are some of the fastest swimmers.
They live in all oceans, in groups of up to 3000. Striped dolphins often jump clear of the water in long, low leaps as they swim at speed. This is called 'porpoising', even when dolphins do it!

▲ The divers on this inflatable boat have a spectacular view of two dolphins leaping. Dolphins can reach fast speeds as they dart through the water.

159

River dolphins

360 Several kinds of dolphin only live in rivers or lakes. Most are rare and face many risks. They include pollution, injury from the propellers of ships, and becoming trapped in fishing nets. Other dangers include being caught as food for humans, or starvation because humans have overfished rivers and lakes.

▼ The Amazon River in South America provides the freshwater habitat (home) for the boto.

▶ As the boto comes to the surface and breathes out, the noise it produces sounds like a human sighing.

361 The boto, or Amazon River dolphin, lives in several rivers in South America. It has a very long, slim, beak-like mouth and grows to about 2 metres in length. It feeds mainly in the early morning and late evening. By day it rests floating on its side, waving one flipper in the air. When the Amazon rainforest floods in the wet season, the boto swims among the huge trees.

362 The World Conservation Union (IUCN) has classified one of Asia's river dolphins as critically endangered. The baiji, or Yangtze dolphin of China, is probably extinct – a survey in 2006 failed to find any specimens in the wild. Two other species, the Indus and Ganges River dolphins, live in Indian rivers. They are grey-brown in colour and grow to about 2 metres in length.

◄ The extinct Yangtze dolphin had a white underside and a pale blue-grey back.

▶ One of the main causes of the baiji's probable extinction is the pollution of Yangtze, by factories along its banks and by farm chemicals seeping into the water.

363 Two kinds of dolphin live in both rivers and the sea, usually staying close to the shore. One is the tucuxi, which is quite small at just 1.5 metres in length. It can be found in the Amazon River and around the northeast coast of South America. The other is the Irrawaddy dolphin, found in the seas and rivers of Southeast Asia, from India to northern Australia. It has a blunt nose and blue-grey skin.

364 The franciscana or La Plata dolphin is a river dolphin that has gone back to the sea. It is similar to river dolphins, but lives in shallow water along the southeast coasts of South America. It can be recognized by its very long, slim, sword-like beak.

Shy and secretive

365 Porpoises are in a different subgroup to whales and dolphins. There are six species that are all found in the sea. Most live in shallow water near to coasts and shores. Porpoises have spade-shaped teeth, whereas dolphins have cone-shaped teeth.

Harbour porpoise

Plump body

Spectacled porpoise

Striking black-and-white pattern

Vaquita

Dark grey back and pale sides

▲ Like other members of the cetacean animal group, porpoises use echolocation to hunt, eating mainly fish and squid.

▼ The finless porpoise, as its name would suggest, lacks a dorsal fin. It is a shy animal that swims in small groups.

366 **The spectacled porpoise has a black ring, surrounded by a white ring, around each eye.** It can be found in the Southern Ocean around the lower tip of South America, and near islands such as the Falklands and South Georgia.

▲ When Dall's porpoise swims quickly through water, a long, narrow spray spurts along its back. It is known as the 'rooster's tail' due to its shape.

367 **The harbour or common porpoise is familiar to sailors around the northern waters.** It has the nickname 'puffing pig' because its blow is rarely seen, but can be heard as a series of loud, short puffs – like a mixture of a snort and a sneeze. It eats a wide range of food, including leftovers thrown from boats.

368 **Dall's porpoise is the largest of the group, at about 2 metres long and 200 kilograms in weight.** It lives along the shores of the North Pacific Ocean. It's a fast and agile swimmer, dashing along at over 50 kilometres an hour. However, it rarely leaps above the surface of the water like other porpoises.

Getting together

369 Whales, dolphins and porpoises breed like most other mammals. A male and female get together and mate. The female becomes pregnant and a baby develops inside her womb. The baby is born through her birth canal, which is a small opening near her tail.

370 When a male and female get together, it is called courtship. They need to find a partner so they can have babies, otherwise they would eventually die out. For hours, they swim together and stroke each other with their flippers and flukes. They may also make noises, like 'love songs'. One of the most amazing is the song of the male humpback whale. He travels through the water making wails, squeals and shrieks in a repeating pattern that lasts for up to 22 hours. Then after a pause, he does it again – just to attract a partner!

371 Baleen whales have babies to fit in with their long journeys, or migrations. They give birth in the tropics, when the water is warm all year. This gives the new baby time to grow and become stronger in warm, calm seas, before the migration to colder waters for summer feeding.

372 Most cetacean mothers are pregnant for about 11 months. When the baby is about one year old, the female can mate again. She can only have a baby every two to three years.

◀ A male humpback sings as he 'hangs' in the water, with his head and tail drooping and flippers dangling down.

373 Breeding narwhals can be dangerous. This is because the males swipe and jab each other with their long 'tusks' to try and become partners for waiting females. The tusk is a very long left upper tooth that grows like a sword with a corkscrew pattern. Usually only the males have a tusk, which can be up to 3 metres in length.

▶ At breeding time male narwhals 'fence' with their tusks. They're competing for a female.

Whale and dolphin babies

374 Most female whales, dolphins and porpoises have one baby at a time. Twins or more are very rare. The baby, called a calf, is usually born tail first. It needs to start breathing air at once. The mother nudges it up to the surface of the water, so it can gasp its first breaths.

▲ This tiny newborn dolphin calf is swimming closely alongside its mother for safety.

375 A new baby stays very close to its mother. She protects it, charging at enemies, such as sharks, large sea lions and seals – and perhaps killer whales.

▼ The young beluga is born dark grey or pinky-grey. It gradually becomes lighter, but it may not take on its all-white colouration until it is more than five years old. This calf is about to suckle milk from its mother.

376 Like other mammals, the mother feeds her baby on her own milk. It is very rich and full of goodness. The calf sucks it from the mother's teat, which is usually hidden under a fold of skin on her underside.

377
Most baby cetaceans feed on their mother's milk for about one year. They grow quickly and soon become strong swimmers. Their mothers teach them how to hunt. By 18 to 24 months of age, the young are independent – able to look after themselves. Baby baleen whales feed on their mother's milk for less time, for only 6 to 8 months.

▼ A female killer whale gives birth to one calf at a time. The mother and baby stay close together until the calf is weaned off its mother's milk.

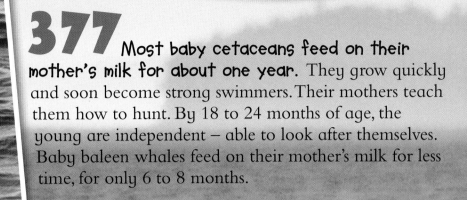

378
It is difficult to know how long whales, dolphins and porpoises live. Scientists can guess their age from the way their teeth grow. Inside the teeth of some species are rings, like the rings in tree trunks. On average, there is one ring for each year of growth. Most dolphins survive for 15 to 25 years. Baleen whales may live for 70 to 80 years. However, some whales and dolphins have been known to survive much longer.

I DON'T BELIEVE IT!
The blue whale calf is the world's biggest baby at 7 metres in length and 3 tonnes in weight. It drinks 350 litres of its mother's milk everyday – enough to fill four bathtubs!

Stories and mysteries

▲ Common dolphins are pictured on the walls of the palaces at Knossos in Crete, which were built by the Minoans about 4000 years ago.

379 **Thousands of years ago cetaceans were greatly admired.** The ancient Greeks and Minoans created pictures and statues of them in their palaces and temples. Whale bones and carvings have been found in the remains of settlements that are 4000 years old, from the Inuits of North America and the Norse people of Northern Europe.

380 **Whales and dolphins feature in many songs, tales and books.** In the Bible, Jonah was swallowed by a whale. Rudyard Kipling wrote a story called *How the Whale Got Its Throat* to explain why the whale has grooves on its throat.

381 *Moby Dick*, **written by Herman Melville in 1851, is one of the best-known whale stories.** It is an adventure tale about Captain Ahab's quest to catch and kill a huge white sperm whale called Moby Dick because it had injured him.

◀ In the novel *Moby Dick*, the giant whale ferociously fights off the sailors who try to hunt him.

382

No one knows for sure why cetaceans can become stranded on shores. Scientists have come up with possible reasons – the animals may be ill, or may have been disturbed by storms or undersea earthquakes. Or they may simply be lost, looking for a way to escape predators.

QUIZ

1. Which whale species is often found stranded?
2. On which Greek island are the ancient palaces at Knossos?
3. What type of whale is Moby Dick in Herman Melville's novel of the same name?

Answers:
1. Pilot whales 2. Crete 3. Sperm whale

383

Among the most common victims of stranding are pilot whales. They live in close groups and have strong bonds with each other. If one whale strays too near the shore, it may become stranded. Other members of the group will often follow it because they don't want to leave the stranded whale alone. They then become stuck on the shore, too. Sometimes more than 50 pilot whales end up stranded.

◀ These people are trying to rescue some stranded pilot whales. It is a tricky task that needs skill and knowledge, and sometimes specialized equipment.

169

The old days of whaling

384 About 1000 years ago, the Basque people from northern Spain began to hunt whales from boats. The hunting spread around Europe, across the Atlantic to North America, then to southern regions like South Africa. By the early 1800s, hundreds of sailing ships were whaling every day. The men used small rowing boats and spears.

▼ In this early 19th-century scene, off the Atlantic coast of North America, a harpooner takes aim at a right whale from his rowing boat. The main hunting boat approaches in the distance.

385 In the mid 1800s, the harpoon gun was invented. It used explosives to fire a harpoon tied to a strong rope, so the whale could be hauled back. Steamships replaced old sailing ships. They could travel further and faster in most weather conditions. The mass slaughter of whales began.

386 By the mid 1900s, whaling fleets were large and well equipped. Catcher boats pursued and harpooned the whales. Their bodies were hauled onto a giant factory ship for processing. However by this time, many areas of the ocean had no whales left. They had all been killed.

387 Whales were used in many ways.
Their fat, oil and blubber went into foods such as margarines, and was burned in lamps. The meat was eaten in some areas, especially eastern Asia. The baleen was used in machinery and for fashion items, such as women's corsets

388 During the 1970s, people around the world began to turn against whaling. It seemed cruel to spear and kill these mammals. Also, many kinds of whale were so rare, they were in danger of being killed off completely.

▲ Whale bones were once used as building materials and tools to make glue and fertilizer.

389 The International Whaling Commission controls the whaling industry. In 1986, it decided to ban mass slaughter of whales, with an international agreement, or moratorium.

390 Some whales have now returned to areas where they had been killed off. Whales breed slowly – females only have one baby every two or three years – so it will take a long time until whales are plentiful in the oceans again.

Working with people

391 Many people visit an aquarium or sea-life centre to see whales, dolphins and porpoises. The most common cetacean kept in captivity is the bottlenose dolphin. Some centres have killer whales and a few even have minke whales. Although they are the smallest of the baleen group, minke whales can still grow up to 10 metres long and 10 tonnes in weight.

WHAT A PERFORMANCE!

You will need:
thick card   scissors   pens or crayons   drinking straw   sticky tape

Draw, cut out and colour a dolphin outline on card. Stick the straw to it, as a handle. Now invent tricks and put on your own show.

392 Dolphins can be interesting creatures to work with. Trainers are able to build a strong bond with them. Dolphins even change tricks or invent new puzzles to make them more fun.

▼ Dolphins can be trained by professionals to perform tricks in return for food. They can learn to leap through hoops and knock balls with their beaks.

▼ At the Dolphin Research Institute in Hawaii, US, researchers study dolphin intelligence. This clever dolphin has correctly recognized a shape it was shown a few minutes before. It indicates its answer by pressing the nearest paddle with its beak.

393
Dolphins are very clever creatures. Studies performed on dolphins in captivity have shown that they are able to correctly recognize shapes and even count.

394
Some people believe all captive dolphins should be set free. The dolphins are sometimes kept in small, bare tanks, with few toys. They may take part in several shows each day and can get bored and tired. They may suffer from loneliness or illness.

395
There are arguments in favour of captive dolphins, too. If several animals live together in a big, safe pool, with plenty of equipment and good food they shouldn't get bored. Spectators can see what amazing animals they are, and learn more about saving wild dolphins.

FAMILY ENTERTAINMENT

FREE WILLY
HOW FAR WOULD YOU GO FOR A FRIEND?

A FRIENDSHIP YOU COULD NEVER IMAGINE.
AN ADVENTURE YOU'LL NEVER FORGET.

▲ Free Willy (1993) told the tale of a boy's quest to set free a performing killer whale. The killer whale that starred in the film was released into the sea near Norway.

Harm and help

396 Most baleen whales are protected by law around the world. Only a small amount of controlled hunting is allowed, although illegal hunting continues in some countries. Conservation parks, such as the Southern Sanctuary in Antarctica, are set aside to protect marine life.

▲ Pilot whales can be found in groups. Unfortunately this makes it easier for whale hunters to catch them.

397 Despite these laws, hunting of whales, dolphins and porpoises still goes on. Some whalers have turned to catching smaller types, such as melon-headed whales and pilot whales. If the hunting continues, they may also face extinction.

398 Whales and dolphins can drown even though they live in water. If they get stuck underwater for some reason, they cannot breathe and may die. One of the greatest dangers for cetaceans is becoming trapped in fishing nets – this causes nearly 1000 to die each day.

▼ This humpback whale is being released back into the ocean after being caught and tangled in a fishing line.

I DON'T BELIEVE IT!

There are stories of people being saved by dolphins when in danger at sea. The dolphin may nudge them to shore. Some people even tell of dolphins protecting them from sharks!

399 **Another hazard for cetaceans is pollution.** Chemicals from coastal factories, power stations and oil refineries wash along rivers into the sea. Some dolphins – especially river dolphins – and porpoises are badly affected because they live near the shore.

400 **Ecotourism is becoming popular.** Tourists take trips on whale-watching boats, or swim with dolphins near the beach. The money made should be used to support wildlife and conservation. In some places this does not happen, and the whales and dolphins are disturbed or frightened. It's a delicate balance between our use of the sea and its creatures, and looking after their environment and well-being.

▼ This group of tourists get an incredible view of a majestic humpback whale breaching near Hawaii.

SHIPWRECKS

401 Originally, the word 'wreck' meant 'something washed up on a seashore'. Today, 'wreck' is used to describe the remains of a ship that has sunk or been badly damaged. In the past, shipwrecks were more common because more people travelled by water, and ships and navigation techniques were less reliable. Today shipwrecks are less frequent, but they still claim thousands of lives each year.

▼ In 1588, Spain sent an Armada (fleet of ships) to attack England, but it was scattered by English fireships (ships set on fire and sent towards enemies), and around half were wrecked in a storm. This painting is called *Defeat of the Spanish Armada*, and was painted by Philippe–Jacques de Loutherbourg in 1797.

How ships float — and sink

402 The Greek scientist Archimedes found out why things float over 2000 years ago. He jumped into his bath and noticed that when he did so, the water overflowed. He realized his body was pushing the water out. When ships float, they 'displace' water, in the same way.

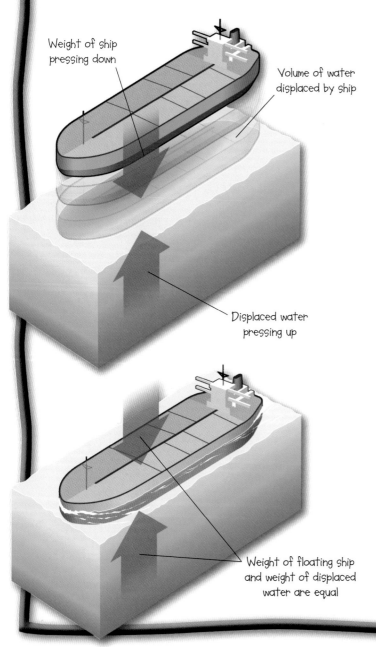

Weight of ship pressing down

Volume of water displaced by ship

Displaced water pressing up

Weight of floating ship and weight of displaced water are equal

◀ The water displaced by a floating ship pushes back with a powerful force equal to the ship's weight.

403 Archimedes discovered that water displaced by a ship pushes back on the ship with a force equal to its weight. This holds the ship up in the water. The density of a ship is also important. Density is the weight of an object measured along with its volume. If a ship or any object is less dense than water, it will float. If it is more dense than water, it will sink.

404 Ships are often made of materials such as iron or steel, which are denser than water. However, ships also contain a lot of air. Air is very light, and makes the ship much less dense than water.

DOES IT FLOAT?

You will need:
bucket, half full of water selection of small objects (pebble, seashell, marble, leaf, coin etc.) pen and paper

1. Make a chart with three columns, headed 'Object', 'Will it float?' and 'Does it float?'.

2. For each object, predict whether you think it will float.

3. Test each object to see whether it floats, and record the answers on your chart.

Did you predict correctly?

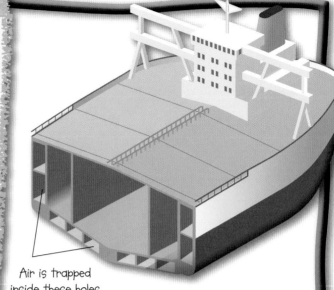

Air is trapped inside these holes

▲ Modern ships have double hulls, which trap air between two layers of metal. Air is less dense than water. The trapped air makes the ship less dense, helping to stop it sinking.

405 Ships sink when water gets inside them. A decrease in the amount of air inside a ship makes it less buoyant. Water gets into ships when they are holed by rocks or guns, battered by winds, swamped by waves, lean sideways too far, or overturn.

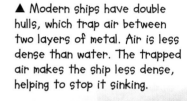

▶ If a ship's hull is holed, water pours in. Together, the hull and the water are denser than water alone, so the ship sinks. This picture shows the oil tanker *Braer*, shipwrecked off the Shetland Islands, off the Scottish coast, in 1993.

Treasures of the deep

◄ A diver scans the seabed, searching for metal objects such as coins or cannon that will help him locate a wreck buried in the sand.

406 Wrecked ships can become trapped on rocks or be washed ashore, but more often they sink beneath the waves. They may sink straight downwards, or twist and turn for many metres before coming to rest. Then they may be crushed by water pressure, pulled apart by currents, or covered by corals, mud and sand.

◄ Divers 'float' above the fragile remains of a shipwreck to examine them before touching or removing them.

407 Investigators search for shipwrecks in many different ways. They look for clues, such as coins or pottery, or strange, unnatural shapes on the seabed. They use echo-sounders and side-scan sonar to 'see' in dark, cloudy water, and magnetometers (electrical detectors) to locate metal objects. Sometimes, they use robots and towed vehicles to make surveys.

408
Before they dive, investigators study maps, charts, ancient books and old newspapers. They read coastguard reports and consult government records of accidents and shipwrecks. They find out about local sea conditions, such as waves and tides, as well as freak weather events such as hurricanes.

409
To reveal a wreck, investigators may make bore-holes through sand and mud, or drill through coral. Sometimes they use pumps to suck mud from above a wreck, or suck sand away with compressed air. Once they get close, they have to work much more carefully. Instead of using tools to brush mud or sand away, they uncover objects by fanning them with their hands.

410
Once a wreck is found, its site is marked with a grid, or poles fixed at regular distances. These help investigators draw plans of the site and record the positions of their finds. Satellite measurements and photographs help record the wreck as it is revealed. All objects taken from the site are labelled, listed, drawn, examined and identified.

◄ Divers use a float filled with air to help raise a heavy iron cannon, found at a 17th century Spanish shipwreck.

I DON'T BELIEVE IT!
Some divers have suggested using sea lions to help explore wrecks. Sea lions are intelligent, and can swim and dive in spaces too small or dangerous for humans to explore.

Diving discoveries

411 People have longed to explore shipwrecks for centuries. Humans can only survive underwater for a short time. They must breathe oxygen, keep their lungs free of water, and be protected from the weight of water above them and from the cold of the seas.

412 For over 500 years, people have tried to design diving suits. In 1715, English inventor John Lethbridge built his 'Diving Engine'. Shaped like a big wooden tube, it had a glass viewing panel and leather sleeves. Divers using it claimed to have explored 18 metres below the surface of the sea.

▲ John Lethbridge's Diving Engine was used in 1718 to collect treasure from the wreck of a ship in the Atlantic Ocean.

▶ Sealing the helmet and suit made diving safer – divers could now be sure of having enough air underwater. Earlier diving suits often filled with water, drowning their wearers. Versions of Siebe's design remained in use until the 1980s.

414 The 'Newt Suit' has been described as 'a submarine you can wear'. Invented in 1987 by Canadian engineer Phil Nuytten, like other ADS (Atmospheric Diving Suit) designs, it surrounds the diver with a metal shell. Inside, the diver is warm, can breathe air at normal pressure, and is not crushed by seawater. He or she can dive to 700 metres, and stay underwater for five or six hours.

413 German engineer Augustus Siebe was called 'the father of diving'. In 1840, he invented a method of sealing together a metal helmet and rubber suit. Air was pumped to the diver down a tube from the surface. In Siebe's suit wearers dived down 25 metres. They explored shipwrecks and built bridges, dams and other underwater constructions.

▶ The Newt Suit is made of strong, light aluminium. Its moveable arms and legs make it easy for divers to work or explore.

Robots and submersibles

415 **Many ships sink in very deep waters.** People cannot safely descend more than 200 metres without protection. They would be crushed by the water pressure, and could not stand the extreme cold. To explore deep sea wrecks, people use robots, towed vehicles, ROVs (remotely-operated vehicles) and submersibles.

▲ Remotely controlled sled ANGUS is fitted with lights and cameras to explore extremely deep seas, and is guided by pilots at sea level.

416 **Robots can be programmed to carry out deep-sea investigations.** Many devices allow robots to collect information about a wreck. Cameras and sonar (scanners that use soundwaves) can create images, sensors test the water, and mechanical arms pick up objects.

▼ ROV *Jason* was launched in 1988. It needs a pilot, a navigator and an engineer to operate it.

417 **ROV *Jason* lets explorers investigate wrecks from sea level.** The mobile unit (*Jason*) is linked to the survey ship by a cable 10 kilometres in length. *Jason* can be steered through a wreck or across the seabed, and can take photos or make and record measurements.

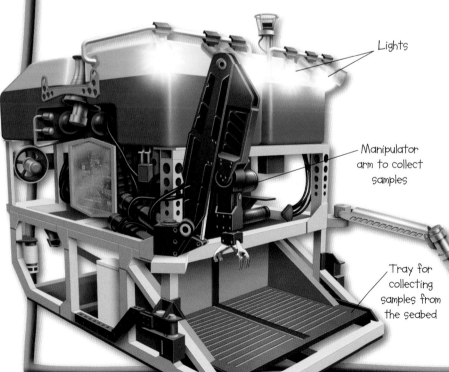

Lights

Manipulator arm to collect samples

Tray for collecting samples from the seabed

Sonar, used to make images of the seabed

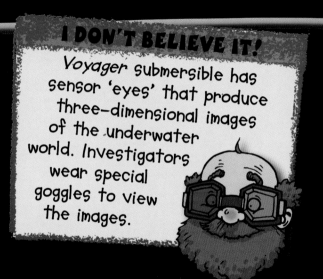

I DON'T BELIEVE IT!

Voyager submersible has sensor 'eyes' that produce three-dimensional images of the underwater world. Investigators wear special goggles to view the images.

419 Towed vehicles can be dragged through deep water by ships sailing on the sea. They are linked to the ship by cables that carry electronic signals. They are used to make maps of wrecks on the seabed, or to take microscopic video images of underwater wildlife and bacteria.

418 *Alvin* was the world's first deep-ocean submersible. Built in 1964, it has completed an astonishing 4200 dives. It is a strong, watertight capsule that can carry two investigators and a pilot 4500 metres below the sea's surface. It is fitted with bright lights, air supply, viewing windows and robot arms, and is propelled by six jet thrusters.

▼ Submersibles need very powerful lights, as it is pitch dark in the ocean depths. Submersibles are smaller than submarines, only carrying a few people to operate them, but they can dive to far greater depths.

The first shipwrecks

420 The earliest wrecks so far discovered are over 3000 years old. They are the remains of two trading ships that sailed the Mediterranean Sea between 1350 BC and 1200 BC. They were both found close to the Turkish coast, at Ulu Burun and Gelidonya. Storms had driven them onto rocks, and sunk them.

421 Both ships' hulls had almost disappeared. Just a few scraps of wood remained. Archaeologists had to estimate their size and shape from cargoes scattered on the sea floor. They also found clues in wall paintings from ancient Egyptian tombs showing Mediterranean ships and traders.

Carved stone seal

▼ The Ulu Burun ship carried gold and silver jewellery, pottery, brilliant blue glass, ivory, valuable ingots (bars) of copper and tin, and many other valuable items.

Wooden writing tablets

422 Cargo on board each ship was packed in giant jars. These huge pots, called 'pithoi', kept cargoes dry and safe. They were stacked at the bottom of a ship's hull, and surrounded by bundles of twigs for padding.

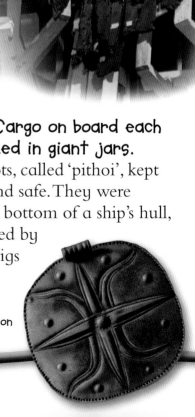

Gold medallion

◀ Archaeologists hard at work cleaning and preserving the wooden hull of the Kyrenia shipwreck.

I DON'T BELIEVE IT!

Divers excavating the Cape Gelidonya wreck had to be tied onto it to prevent them being swept away by currents!

423 Sailors on the Cape Gelidonya ship carried charms for protection. Five stone scarabs have been found at the wreck, along with the ship-owner's merchant seal. This was a little cylinder, carved with symbols, used to stamp the merchant's signature on bundles of cargo.

▼ Experts built a copy of the Kyrenia ship in 1985, so they could find out more about ancient Greek ships and how they were sailed.

424 In 1967, divers discovered wreckage on the seabed near Kyrenia, Cyprus. It was the remains of a Greek cargo ship that sank over 2300 years ago. Amazingly, three-quarters of the wooden hull remained, and was almost undamaged!

425 Hundreds more ancient wrecks have been discovered in the Mediterranean. They date from ancient Greek and Roman times, between around 500 BC and AD 500. The wrecked ships carried all kinds of valuable cargoes, from wine and olive oil to works of art – and slaves.

Viking shipwrecks

426 The Skudelev ships were discovered in Denmark in 1959. They lay across Roskilde Fjord (a long, thin bay), completely blocking the narrow entrance. They had been wrecked on purpose around AD 1000 to prevent enemy ships approaching. Their hulls had been filled with heavy stones to stop them floating to the surface.

▶ Danish Vikings sinking the Skudelev ships to make an underwater barrier against invaders. The wrecks stayed hidden underwater for nearly 1000 years.

Sunken ship on shallow sea floor

427 Investigating the wrecks was difficult and delicate. The timbers were so fragile that they could not be moved through the water. So the archaeologists built a coffer dam – like a box in the sea – and pumped the water out of it. Then they carefully lifted the wrecked ships to the surface, piece by piece.

Ship being filled with stones before sinking

428 Reconstructing the wrecks was like piecing together a puzzle, and took many years. Over 50,000 pieces of wood were found in the fjord. Each was photographed and numbered before being moved. Now they are on show in a museum.

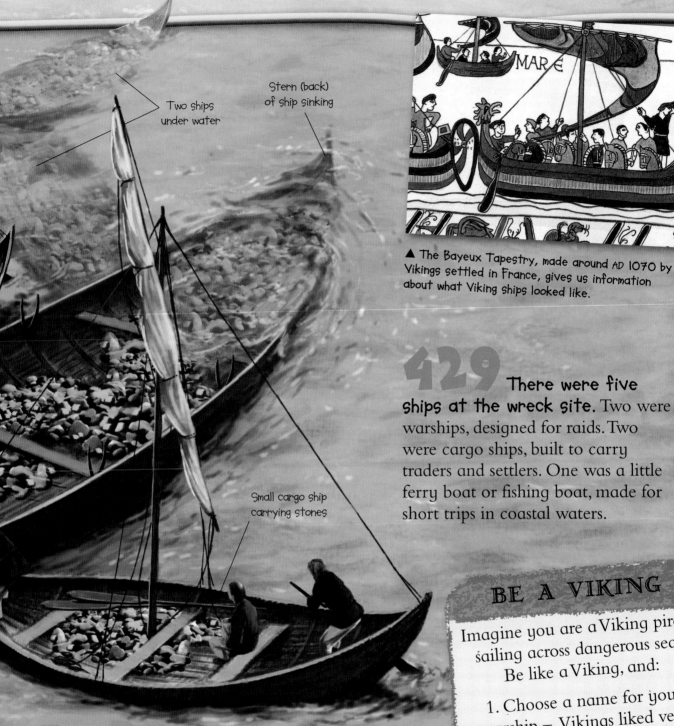

Two ships under water

Stern (back) of ship sinking

Small cargo ship carrying stones

▲ The Bayeux Tapestry, made around AD 1070 by Vikings settled in France, gives us information about what Viking ships looked like.

429 **There were five ships at the wreck site.** Two were warships, designed for raids. Two were cargo ships, built to carry traders and settlers. One was a little ferry boat or fishing boat, made for short trips in coastal waters.

430 **Ships like the Skudelev warship carried invaders.** They are pictured in the Bayeux Tapestry, a huge embroidered wall-hanging that records the Norman Conquest of Britain in 1066. Ships like the Skudelev cargo ship reached North America around AD 1000, steered by Viking explorers.

BE A VIKING

Imagine you are a Viking pirate, sailing across dangerous seas. Be like a Viking, and:

1. Choose a name for your warship – Vikings liked very descriptive names such as 'Wave-Beater' or 'Sea-Snake'.

2. Write a poem or a song, describing your hopes and fears for your voyage. Will your journey bring you fame and riches, or will it end in a dramatic shipwreck?

Medieval Europe

▲ Galleys smashed holes in enemy ships with sharp battering rams. They also hurled 'bombs' of an explosive mixture called Greek Fire.

431 **The Pisa wreck was lost for over 700 years.** It was a galley (a ship with oars and sails) belonging to merchants from the city of Pisa in Italy. Medieval writers described how the ship was attacked by rivals in 1277, off the coast of Ukraine. It was set on fire, overturned, and sank to the bottom of the Black Sea. For centuries, no one knew where it was, but in 1999, archaeologists found it!

432 **On board was lots of fancy pottery made for rich Italian families.** Italian people of the time were able to buy beautiful things imported from distant lands. Bowls and dishes found at the wreck site were made by potters working in several different styles and traditions. Some were Christians, from Constantinople (now Istanbul and Turkey). Others were Muslims from the Middle East.

▶ The big wooden hull of the Bremen cog is 15.5 metres in length. Amazingly, it was still in one piece when it was found.

MAKE A PENDANT

You will need:
clay   gold paint   paintbrush   ribbon

1. Shape a disk of clay 4 centimetres across and half a centimetre thick.

2. Press a ship design into the disk, and make a hole at the top.

3. Leave to dry, then paint with the gold paint and leave to dry again.

4. Thread the ribbon through the hole. Your pendant is ready to wear!

▶ Combining evidence from shipwrecks with images like this medieval seal allows archaeologists to work out what the Bremen Cog might have looked like over 600 years ago.

434 **Few medieval shipwrecks survive.** The wood, hemp fibre and canvas they were made of has rotted away. One of the best-preserved medieval wrecks is the Bremen Cog, from Germany. It was found in 1962, by dredgers (digging machines) widening a harbour entrance.

433 **One kind of pot that was found on the Pisa wreck is a mystery.** Called a 'spheroconus', it is shaped like a globe with a spout. It may have been used to store mercury – a poisonous medieval medicine – or water from Mecca, the Muslim holy city. Or it might have been a weapon to throw at enemy ships!

435 **The Bremen Cog was wrecked before it ever set sail.** Around 1380, floods swept it from a ship-builder's yard. After being stranded on a sandbank, it became covered with mud and silt. This stopped bacteria from rotting its timbers.

Chinese junks

436 **Chinese junks were the biggest ocean-going sailing ships in the world.** We know this from Chinese shipwrecks. In 1973, a wrecked junk was discovered near Quanzhou, south China. It was 34 metres in length and 11 metres in width and could carry 350 tonnes. It had three tall masts and was five times bigger than most European ships of its time.

437 **Junks had special features that made them unlikely to sink.** They had bulkheads (walls), which divided their hulls into compartments. Each compartment had a watertight cover and a drainage channel.

438 **The Quanzhou junk was wrecked around 1275, probably in a typhoon (hurricane).** It was blown onto rocks, a huge hole was smashed in its hull, and all the compartments filled with water. Accidents like this show that even the best-designed ships cannot always survive the very worst weather.

439 Lucky charms were hidden on junks for extra protection at sea. Divers exploring the Quanzhou wreck found seven bronze coins and a mirror. These represented the moon and the stars – traditional Chinese symbols of fair winds and good fortune.

440 Around 60 merchants sailed on the Quanzhou wreck. Each had his own cabin. They were travelling with precious cargoes from Africa and South Asia, including pepper, perfumes, tortoiseshell and seashells (which they used like coins). Other junks carried spices and fine pottery.

◄ A Chinese junk, similar to the Quanzhou junk, is blown across the sea by a violent typhoon. The sailors struggle to lower its sails to reduce its speed through the water. Waves surge around the hull, but its waterproof design helps it stay afloat, unless it is holed.

Tudor ship

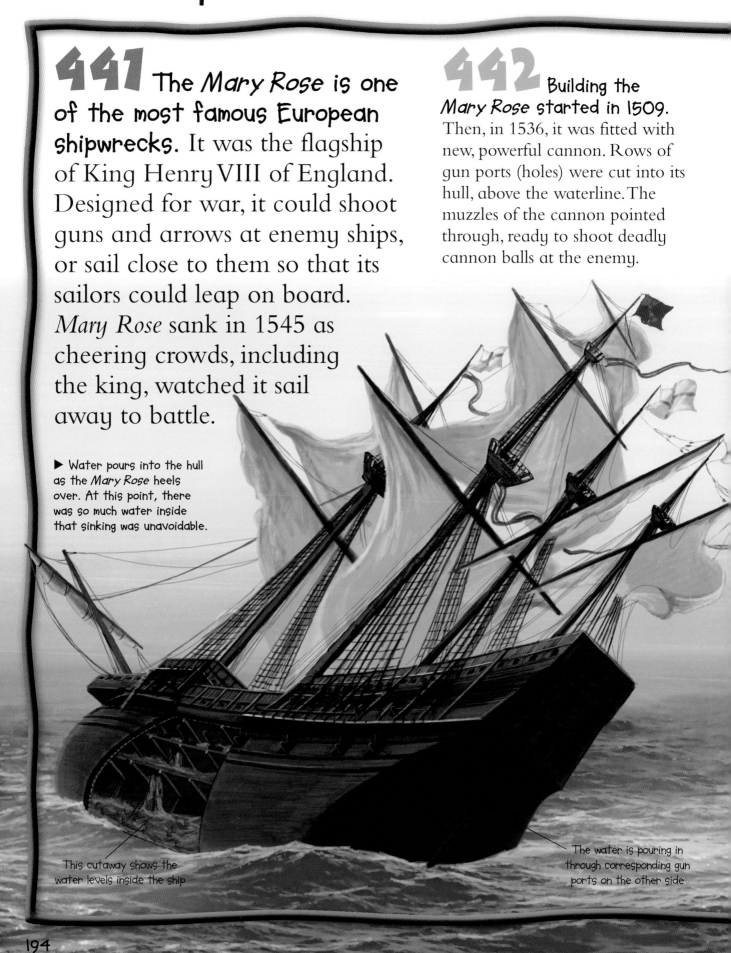

441 The *Mary Rose* is one of the most famous European shipwrecks. It was the flagship of King Henry VIII of England. Designed for war, it could shoot guns and arrows at enemy ships, or sail close to them so that its sailors could leap on board. *Mary Rose* sank in 1545 as cheering crowds, including the king, watched it sail away to battle.

▶ Water pours into the hull as the *Mary Rose* heels over. At this point, there was so much water inside that sinking was unavoidable.

442 Building the *Mary Rose* started in 1509. Then, in 1536, it was fitted with new, powerful cannon. Rows of gun ports (holes) were cut into its hull, above the waterline. The muzzles of the cannon pointed through, ready to shoot deadly cannon balls at the enemy.

This cutaway shows the water levels inside the ship

The water is pouring in through corresponding gun ports on the other side

▲ Slowly and very carefully, the wreck of the *Mary Rose* is lifted from the seabed on a massive metal cradle that has been specially made in exactly the same shape as the ship's hull.

443 The weight of people and guns on the upper decks made the *Mary Rose* unstable.
Suddenly, it heeled (leaned over) to one side and water poured in through its gun ports. It could not right itself (return to an upright, balanced position), filled with water, and sank rapidly. The soldiers and sailors on board were trapped by nets meant to keep out enemies. Around 500 drowned.

444 The *Mary Rose* came to rest leaning on its starboard (right-hand) side.
Its starboard decks and cabins sank unharmed into the soft mud of the seabed, close to Portsmouth, southern England. Year by year, layers of silt covered the wreck, hiding it completely. The *Mary Rose* became a secret Tudor time capsule.

445 Investigators have tried to explore the *Mary Rose* wreck several times.
Soon after it sank, Italian experts tried to find its valuable cannon. Between 1836 and 1840, divers dropped explosives near the wreck to uncover it. Archaeologists surveyed the wreck in 1967, then began to excavate it in 1979. In 1982, the remains of the *Mary Rose* were lifted to the surface. Today, they are displayed in a museum.

I DON'T BELIEVE IT!

In just four years, from 1979 to 1983, archaeologists made almost 25,000 dives to the seabed to recover the shipwrecked *Mary Rose* and its contents.

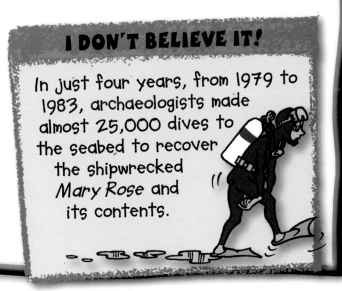

East India ships

446 **The *Batavia* was one of the first sailing ships to sink off Australia.** Owned by a Dutch trading company, it ran aground on reefs between Australia and Indonesia. The dangerous seas in this area sank hundreds of similar ships, called East Indiamen, between 1600 and 1800.

447 **At first, it took a year for an East Indiaman to sail from Europe to Indonesia.** In 1613, Dutch captain Hendrick Brouwer pioneered a new route across the south Indian Ocean. This made use of reliable 'trade' winds, and reduced the journey time by half to around six months at sea. The *Batavia* was following this route when she was wrecked in 1629.

448 **We know a lot about the *Batavia* wreck because the captain survived.** He wrote a description of the ship hitting rocks – and what happened afterwards. With some officers, he set off in small a boat to seek help, leaving 268 passengers and crew sheltering on the islands. After they had left, a passenger and his friends attacked the other survivors.

◀ Strong gales and wild waves washed the *Batavia* onto hidden rocky reefs. With only wind to power their ship, its crew were powerless to avoid them.

▶ Archaeologists investigating the East Indiamen wrecks carefully record the positions of anchors, cannon – and boxes of treasure.

449 The *Batavia* mutineers killed 125 men, women and children. No one knows why. Perhaps they feared they would run out of food and water. When the captain returned with rescuers, after an adventurous voyage, the murderers were executed.

450 The wreck of the *Batavia* was discovered in 1963. It had sunk into a shallow reef and was overgrown by coral. This protected it and its contents from being scattered or swept away by waves and currents. Guns, anchors, ballast and parts of the hull all lay on the seabed in almost the same positions as when the ship was sailing.

I DON'T BELIEVE IT!

The 'trade' winds, used by ships like the *Batavia*, got their name because they always blow along the same path across the ocean.

▶ Sailors on board the *Batavia* used astrolabes to measure time and try to calculate how far they had travelled eastwards. Accurate clocks that worked at sea had not yet been invented.

451 Surprising things were found at the *Batavia* wreck site. These included a set of silver dishes for the Indian Emperor Jehangir and a carved stone doorway for the Dutch fort at Batavia (now Jakarta, Indonesia). Also found were four astrolabes (instruments used to plot a ship's position) and part of a globe showing the countries of the world known to Europeans around 1600.

Pirate wrecks

452 Spanish settlers in America sent gold and silver home to Spain, but many of their ships were robbed by pirates, wrecked on reefs or sunk by hurricanes. Only two pirate shipwrecks have been found. One is the *Whydah*, the other is the *Queen Anne's Revenge*.

453 The *Whydah* was launched in 1715 in London, England. It was named after the West African port, Ouidah (pronounced 'Whee-dah'). It was 31 metres in length, and needed a crew of 146 men. The *Whydah* was captured by the pirate Samuel Bellamy, known as 'Black Sam' because of his dark hair.

▶ Pirate captain 'Black Sam' Bellamy was only 29 years old when he drowned in the wreck of his ship *Whydah*.

BE A PIRATE

You will need:
square of bright red cloth

1. Fold the cloth in half.

2. Stretch the long side of the cloth across your forehead.

3. Tie the points of the cloth at the back of your head. Now you're ready to sail the stormy seas!

▶ Bellamy's loot, stored on the *Whydah*, included 180 sacks of gold and silver jewellery and bullion (pieces of gold and silver metal), and more than 100,000 gold coins.

454 Heading home to London in 1717 after its second slave-trade voyage, the *Whydah* met Bellamy. He chased it for three days then captured it. He then sailed the *Whydah* northwards, along America's east coast, robbing 53 ships he met along the way. The pirate crew on the *Whydah* came from many different lands including Britain, America, Africa and the Caribbean.

455 The *Whydah* sailed into a storm off Cape Cod in 1717. It was battered by 112-kilometre-an-hour winds and 9-metre-high waves. Bellamy tried to steer the ship away from the shore, but it hit a sandbank. It overturned, and smashed into pieces. All but eight of the crew drowned. When the survivors got to shore they were arrested and six were executed for their pirate crimes.

456 The *Queen Anne's Revenge* belonged to the pirate Edward Teach. He was known as 'Blackbeard' because he wore burning fuses under his hat to surround his face with smoke. In 1718, Blackbeard and his crew attacked the port of Charleston, South Carolina, USA, but were chased and fought by a British Navy ship. Blackbeard was killed, and the *Queen Anne's Revenge* sank near Charleston.

Ship's graveyard

457 The seas around Cape Horn, the southern tip of South America, are the wildest in the world. Fast currents, rocky shores, thick fogs, icebergs, roaring winds and massive waves up to 30 metres high make sailing difficult and very dangerous. There are 78 known wrecks charted at Cape Horn itself, with at least 800 more in the seas nearby.

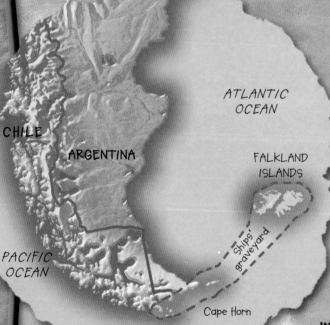

ATLANTIC OCEAN

CHILE

ARGENTINA

FALKLAND ISLANDS

Ships' graveyard

PACIFIC OCEAN

Cape Horn

▲ The seas around Cape Horn and between Cape Horn and the Falkland Islands became known as the 'ships' graveyard' because so many great sailing ships were wrecked there.

458 Why did sailors and ship-owners risk these dangerous waters? To make money! In the early 19th century, before railways were built in the USA, the quickest way to reach California was to sail round Cape Horn. In 1848, gold was discovered there. The next year, 777 ships sailed round Cape Horn, carrying eager gold miners.

◀ The ships that raced around Cape Horn were fast 'clippers', with slim, streamlined hulls, up to 12 metres wide and 60 metres in length. Clippers needed big crews – about 50 men – to handle their massive sails. Steering clippers was a skilled and exhausting task.

I DON'T BELIEVE IT!

A sailor who had sailed round Cape Horn was allowed to wear a gold hoop in his left ear. Some sailors said grimly that the gold would pay for their funerals.

459 In 1912, the British sailing ship *Cricceth Castle* set sail from Peru towards Europe. It was loaded with guano – dried sea bird droppings, which were to be used as fertilizer. As the *Cricceth Castle* rounded Cape Horn, its rudder was smashed in a storm, letting water into the hold. This mixed with the guano and blocked the ship's pumps completely. The hold flooded, and the *Cricceth Castle* sank. Only seven sailors survived.

460 Clipper ships also sailed from Australia and New Zealand. They carried wool, grain and gold to Britain. In 1890, New Zealand clipper the *Marlborough* was wrecked on its way to the Scottish port of Glasgow. The next year, another clipper crew saw the *Marlborough* on rocks near Cape Horn. They sailed closer, and saw skeletons on board! The *Marlborough*'s crew must have starved to death after their ship was wrecked.

Civil War wreck

461 Between 1861 and 1865, the USA fought a civil war. Northern states fought Southern states over trade and slavery. Important battles were fought at sea, as Northern ships blockaded (closed off) Southern ports to stop the South selling its produce. Many ships on both sides were wrecked. One of the most famous was the Northern 'iron-clad', *USS Hatteras*.

▼ The ship that wrecked the *Hatteras* was the *CSS Alabama*. It was one of the the most famous, and deadly, ships of the Civil War. As well sinking the *Hatteras*, the *Alabama* captured over 60 Northern trading ships. Most were set on fire, then sunk.

462 The *Hatteras* was a new ship, driven by a new invention – steam power. Coal-fired boilers below its deck heated water to make steam. This steam powered an engine that turned two large wheels, one on either side of its hull. These drove the ship through the water.

I DON'T BELIEVE IT!

One year after it wrecked the *Hatteras*, the *Alabama* fought another Northern warship. The shells it fired failed to explode and just bounced off the enemy ship's hull.

463 New materials were used to build the *Hatteras*, as well. It was called an iron-clad because its 60-metre hull was covered in thick iron plates, designed to survive blows from exploding shells and firebombs. Its paddle wheels were also made of iron, and so were its engine and boilers.

464

In the Civil War the *Hatteras* was fitted with five cannon. It patrolled Southern state coasts, capturing seven Southern warships. In 1863, it sighted a sailing ship and hailed it. The ship said it was British, and invited the *Hatteras* crew to visit. The crew launched a boat, climbed in, and then the mystery ship fired its cannon! It was a disguised southern warship. In spite of its plating, *Hatteras* was holed, and sank in 13 minutes.

465

The wreck of the *Hatteras* has survived with very little damage. Unlike earlier wooden ships, its iron hull, boiler and paddle-wheels have not rotted away or been devoured by wood-eating ship-worms. Divers discovered its wreck around 1970. Since then, the greatest threat of damage to the *Hatteras* has come from oil-drilling rigs nearby.

▲ As soon as he recognized the trick played by the *Alabama*, the captain of the *Hatteras* gave orders to fire his ship's guns. He was too late — the *Hatteras* was already sinking.

Ocean liners

466 The *Lusitania* was a luxury ocean liner owned by the Cunard shipping line. Built in Clydebank, Scotland and launched in 1906, it was designed to carry passengers between Britain and New York. In 1907 it won the prestigious 'Blue Riband' award for the fastest Atlantic crossing.

▲ Survivors crowded into small lifeboats look on in horror as the mighty *Lusitania* sinks beneath the waves.

467 In 1914, Britain and Germany went to war. In 1915, the German Embassy in the USA warned travellers that Germany would treat all British ships as enemy targets. The Germans would even attack passenger ships, like the *Lusitania*, that had nothing to do with the British army or navy.

468 The Captain of the *Lusitania* believed that it was safe from attack at sea. It could travel much faster than other ships, even German U-Boats (submarines). Surely, nothing could catch it?

► The sinking of the *Lusitania* was headline news around the world. Readers were shocked by the massive loss of life, and by the attack on unarmed civilians.

QUIZ

1. Where did the *Lusitania* sail?
2. Why did the *Lusitania's* captain think it was safe from attack?
3. What kind of ship wrecked the *Lusitania*?

Answers:
1. Between Britain and the USA
2. It could sail very fast
3. A submarine

471 Just 18 minutes after it was torpedoed, the *Lusitania* sank. Of the 1959 people on board, 1198 died. People around the world protested at this murder of civilians. A few months later, the German government called off all submarine attacks.

469 By chance, the *Lusitania* sailed close to a German submarine off the south coast of Ireland in May 1915. The submarine fired one torpedo. It hit the *Lusitania*, destroying its controls and causing an explosion. Seawater flooded in and the *Lusitania* keeled over.

470 There were 48 lifeboats on the *Lusitania*, but only six reached the sea. Many could not be launched because the ship was tilting over. Some lifeboats were damaged by huge rivets fastening parts of the hull and others overturned as sailors tried to lower them.

▶ The US government used images of drowned women and children to encourage men to enlist (join the army or navy) to fight against Germany during World War I (1914–1918).

ENLIST

Fred Spear

Bombs and torpedoes

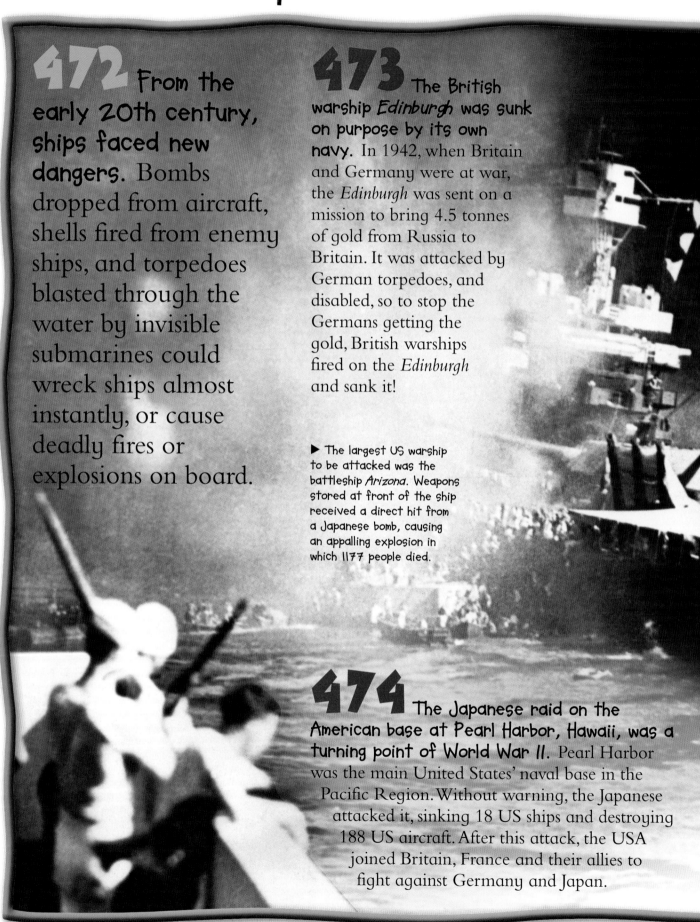

472 From the early 20th century, ships faced new dangers. Bombs dropped from aircraft, shells fired from enemy ships, and torpedoes blasted through the water by invisible submarines could wreck ships almost instantly, or cause deadly fires or explosions on board.

473 The British warship *Edinburgh* was sunk on purpose by its own navy. In 1942, when Britain and Germany were at war, the *Edinburgh* was sent on a mission to bring 4.5 tonnes of gold from Russia to Britain. It was attacked by German torpedoes, and disabled, so to stop the Germans getting the gold, British warships fired on the *Edinburgh* and sank it!

▶ The largest US warship to be attacked was the battleship *Arizona*. Weapons stored at front of the ship received a direct hit from a Japanese bomb, causing an appalling explosion in which 1177 people died.

474 The Japanese raid on the American base at Pearl Harbor, Hawaii, was a turning point of World War II. Pearl Harbor was the main United States' naval base in the Pacific Region. Without warning, the Japanese attacked it, sinking 18 US ships and destroying 188 US aircraft. After this attack, the USA joined Britain, France and their allies to fight against Germany and Japan.

QUIZ

1. What disabled HMS *Edinburgh*?
2. What sank and wrecked USS *Arizona*?
3. What happened after the attack on Pearl Harbor?

Answers:
1. Torpedoes 2. Bombs 3. The USA joined Britain and its allies to fight in World War II

475 The attack on Pearl Harbor took place on 7 December 1941. American ships and planes were attacked by 353 Japanese aircraft, launched from six aircraft carriers patrolling the Pacific Ocean. The planes dropped high-explosive bombs, designed to smash through warships' armour plating. At the same time, five Japanese midget submarines fired torpedoes towards American ships from underneath the sea.

476 The raid on Pearl Harbor caused terrible loss of life. In total, 2388 Americans and their allies were killed and 1178 were injured. Today, the dead are honoured by a fine memorial, built out at sea above the wreck of the sunken US battleship *Arizona*. It lies undisturbed, as a peaceful grave for war victims.

▼ The wreck of the USS *Arizona* can be seen as a ghostly shape through the clear water of Pearl Harbor. The large white building is a memorial to all who were on board.

Shipwrecks today

477 Computers, electronics and scientific design make today's ships safer than ever before. Wrecks still happen though, often through human error. In 2002, the ferry *Joola* sunk off Senegal due to overcrowding. Over 1900 passengers died. In 2007, the *Pasha Bulker* (bulk carrier) was washed ashore in a storm in Australia despite shipping advice to seek safer waters.

478 Mechanical failures still cause tragedies. In 1994, the ferry *Estonia* sank in the Baltic Sea, after locks failed on its bow visor (lifting door) and water flooded in. In total, 852 passengers died. In 2000, the Russian submarine *Kursk* sank with all its crew trapped on board because an experimental torpedo misfired. In spite of efforts to rescue them, all the *Kursk* crew died.

◀ Spills from shipwrecks can kill. Sea birds' feathers become matted with oil, so that they can no longer swim or fly. Fish and other sea creatures are poisoned, and beaches polluted.

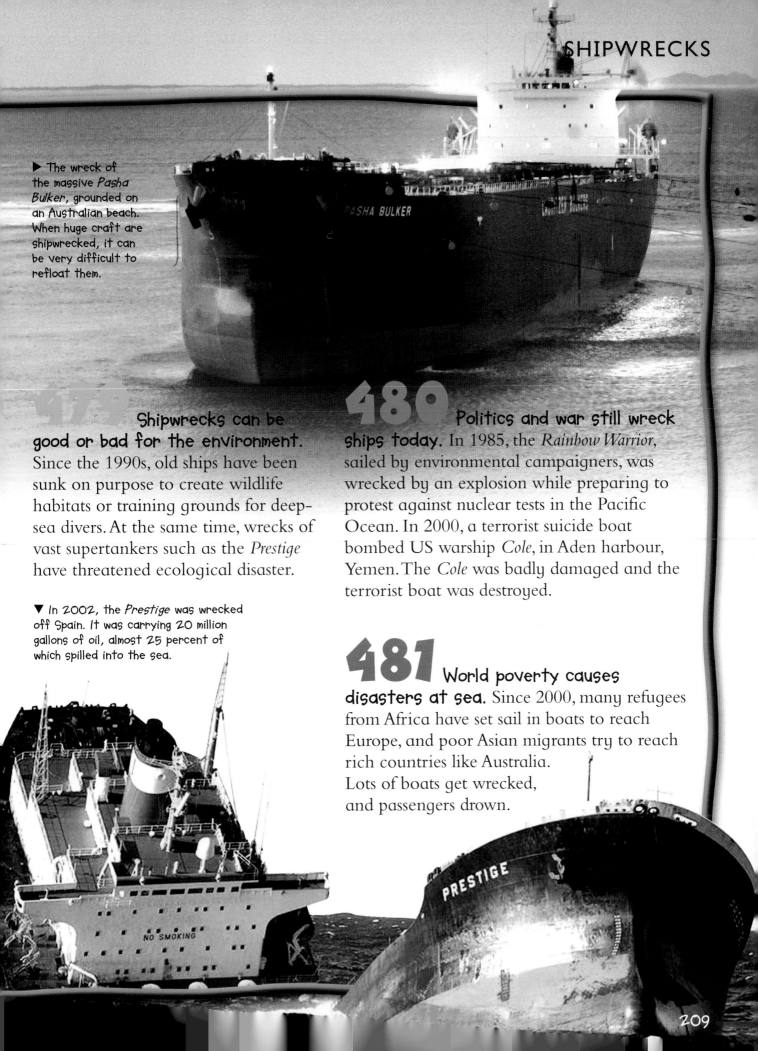

▶ The wreck of the massive *Pasha Bulker*, grounded on an Australian beach. When huge craft are shipwrecked, it can be very difficult to refloat them.

479 Shipwrecks can be good or bad for the environment. Since the 1990s, old ships have been sunk on purpose to create wildlife habitats or training grounds for deep-sea divers. At the same time, wrecks of vast supertankers such as the *Prestige* have threatened ecological disaster.

▼ In 2002, the *Prestige* was wrecked off Spain. It was carrying 20 million gallons of oil, almost 25 percent of which spilled into the sea.

480 Politics and war still wreck ships today. In 1985, the *Rainbow Warrior*, sailed by environmental campaigners, was wrecked by an explosion while preparing to protest against nuclear tests in the Pacific Ocean. In 2000, a terrorist suicide boat bombed US warship *Cole*, in Aden harbour, Yemen. The *Cole* was badly damaged and the terrorist boat was destroyed.

481 World poverty causes disasters at sea. Since 2000, many refugees from Africa have set sail in boats to reach Europe, and poor Asian migrants try to reach rich countries like Australia. Lots of boats get wrecked, and passengers drown.

Survivors and rescuers

482 Shipwrecks can make great stories — if you survive to tell your tale! In 1815, the *Commerce*, a merchant ship from the USA, was wrecked off West Africa. The crew swam ashore, but were captured and made to work as slaves in the Sahara Desert. They managed to escape, and when they got home, they wrote a best-selling book about their experiences!

▶ The *Endurance* was trapped by ice as the ocean froze at the end of the Antarctic summer. Its hull was crushed between ice-floes.

483 In 1915, the British ship Endurance was trapped and crushed by ice in the South Atlantic Ocean, close to the South Pole. This shipwreck left Antarctic explorer Ernest Shackleton and his crew stranded in barren, freezing terrain. For 10 months, they camped on the ice, until the Endurance finally sank.

▼ On Elephant Island, Shackleton and his men built a camp, using their boats as shelters. They survived on food they had managed to save from the wreck of the *Endurance*.

484 Shackleton and his crew faced certain death unless they tried to leave the ice. In April 1916, they set off in three small boats, and reached tiny, remote Elephant Island, off the coast of Antarctica. From there, Shackleton and five brave sailors set off across the wild, stormy ocean, heading for South America.

I DON'T BELIEVE IT!

Ships in danger use a distress call that is recognized internationally. It is 'Mayday! Mayday!'. It comes from the French: 'M'aidez!' which means 'Help me!'

485 After 16 dangerous days, Shackleton and his men reached South Georgia, 1300 kilometres from Elephant Island. They scrambled ashore, and trekked overland to reach a small port used by whaling ships. Once they had recovered from their adventure, they returned to rescue their shipmates. Once safely back in Britain, Shackleton was a hero.

486 The steamship *Admella* hit rocks around the south coast of Australia in 1859. In sight of land but surrounded by raging seas, it sank in 15 minutes, leaving 108 men, women and children clinging to rocks. Rescuers took over a week to reach them. By that time 89 people had died from hunger, cold, thirst, exhaustion or falling into the sea. Only 19 survived.

▼ Shackleton left most of his crew behind on Elephant Island. They were furious, and feared that they would die, but all of them were rescued. Amazingly, no one on Shackleton's expedition died.

Shipwreck stories

487 Tales of shipwrecks have been popular for centuries. One of the first to be written down was the *Odyssey*, in ancient Greece, around 800 BC. It tells the story of a brave Greek hero, Odysseus, who survives witches, giants, monsters – and shipwrecks – on his way home from a war.

I DON'T BELIEVE IT!

Stories of the Kraken – a huge sea-monster that wrecked ships – may have been based on giant squid from Viking waters.

▼ On his travels, Odysseus and his shipmates were surrounded by the Sirens. These were beautiful, half-women, half-bird monsters that sang sweetly, trying to lure sailors towards deadly rocks where their ships would be wrecked and they would drown.

489 Many famous films feature shipwrecks. Classics such as *The Cruel Sea* (Ealing Studios, 1953), portray the the bravery of sailors facing drowning. Adventure films, such as *Poseidon* (Warner Bros. Pictures, 2006) tell stories of ships that are wrecked by freak natural disasters, such as giant ocean waves.

490 The exciting story of a shipwrecked sailor, *Robinson Crusoe* was written by Daniel Defoe in 1719. It tells how Crusoe survived alone on a desert island, building a house from wrecked ship's timbers. The book was based on the real adventures of Scottish runaway and pirate Alexander Selkirk, who was marooned (put ashore as a punishment) on a Pacific Ocean island in 1704, then rescued in 1709.

488 This shipwreck poem is scary. *The Rime of the Ancient Mariner*, written by Samuel Taylor Coleridge in 1798, tells the tale of an old sailor who shoots an albatross (sea bird) that flies beside his ship. As a punishment, he is shipwrecked and endures terrible hunger and thirst. He is also tormented by nightmare visions of 'slimy things' that 'crawl with legs upon the slimy sea'.

▶ In Daniel Defoe's story, Crusoe is washed up on the shore of a wild, uninhabited island, the only survivor of a terrible shipwreck.

213

Shipwreck mysteries

491 Many ships are wrecked far from land, and some are never found. People try to explain these disappearances with stories. The strangest concern the 'Bermuda Triangle', an area of the Atlantic Ocean where over 500 ships are said to have been wrecked mysteriously.

▼ The mysterious Bermuda Triangle is said to stretch from the island of Bermuda to the Florida coast of the USA and the north Caribbean region.

492 The Bermuda Triangle is rumoured to contain time warps, UFOs and extra-terrestrials. It is actually no more perilous than any other stretch of water. However it is very busy, so many ships are wrecked there by hurricanes, powerful waves and strong currents.

493 Sudden freak waves off the tip of South Africa are thought to have caused many shipwrecks. In 1909, the Australian steamship *Waratah* disappeared there, without trace. All 211 passengers on board were never seen again. After several searches, the *Waratah*'s remains still have not been found.

ATLANTIC OCEAN

BERMUDA

FLORIDA

BERMUDA TRIANGLE

BAHAMAS

CUBA

DOMINICAN REPUBLIC

1 In 1812 the *Patriot* vanished off Florida. It was probably sunk by pirates. All the passengers disappeared.

2 In 1864 the *Mari Celeste* sank near Bermuda.

3 In 1918 the warship USS *Cyclops* disappeared. The disappearance is believed to be the result of a storm or enemy action, and the entire crew of 306 were lost.

4 In 1921 the *Carroll A Deering*, a five-masted sailing ship, was found abandoned off Florida. It was probably attacked by rival smugglers.

5 In 1963 the massive tanker SS *Marine Sulphur Queen* disappeared off Florida. However this was not really surprising, as it was badly maintained and unseaworthy.

494 In 1974, the *Gaul* sank suddenly in icy weather off Russia. It was a large British trawler. People thought that the *Gaul* might have been sunk by the Russian navy for spying, or dragged to the bottom of the sea by a Russian submarine. In 2002, a survey of the *Gaul*'s wreck showed that it had probably filled with water in rough seas after waste hatches had been left open.

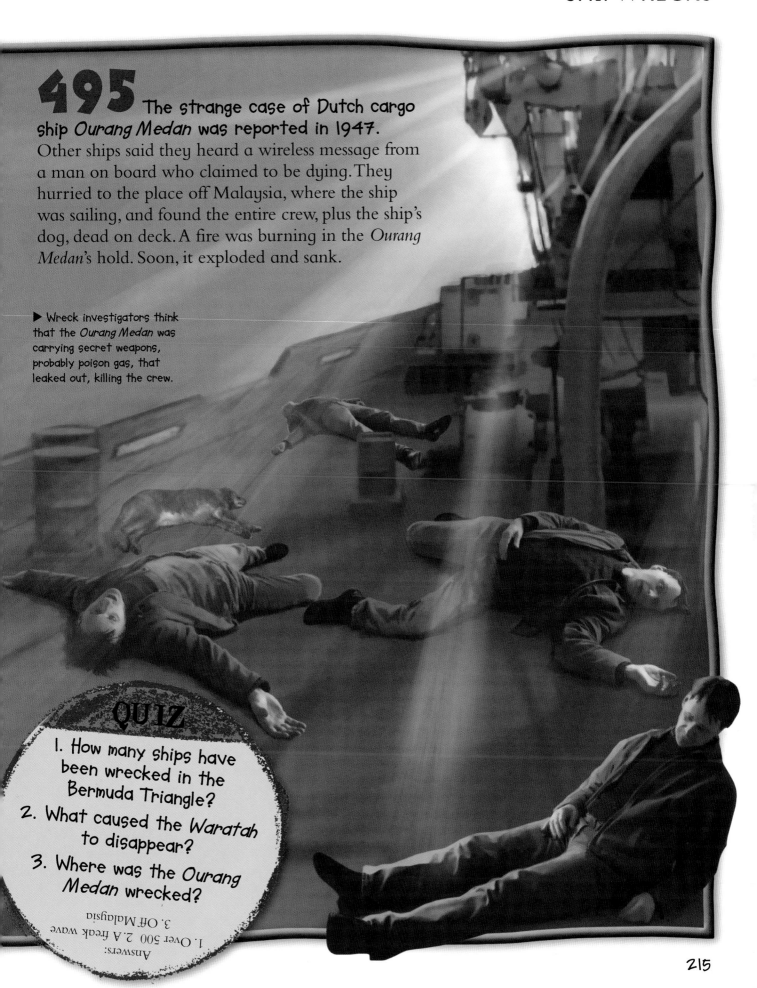

495

The strange case of Dutch cargo ship *Ourang Medan* was reported in 1947. Other ships said they heard a wireless message from a man on board who claimed to be dying. They hurried to the place off Malaysia, where the ship was sailing, and found the entire crew, plus the ship's dog, dead on deck. A fire was burning in the *Ourang Medan*'s hold. Soon, it exploded and sank.

▶ Wreck investigators think that the *Ourang Medan* was carrying secret weapons, probably poison gas, that leaked out, killing the crew.

QUIZ

1. How many ships have been wrecked in the Bermuda Triangle?
2. What caused the *Waratah* to disappear?
3. Where was the *Ourang Medan* wrecked?

Answers:
1. Over 500 2. A freak wave 3. Off Malaysia

The most famous shipwreck

▶ The *Titanic* was 269 metres in length and 28 metres wide. It was propelled by two massive steam engines, powered by 29 steam boilers.

496 The most famous shipwreck is the British ocean liner, RMS *Titanic*. When it was wrecked in 1912 it was the largest, most glamorous passenger ship ever built. It had restaurants, a swimming pool, squash courts and a ballroom.

497 *Titanic*'s designers said it was 'unsinkable'. The hull was double-bottomed and it had bulkheads, but these were shorter than they should have been to make extra space for first class passengers. This meant water could pour over the top of them and sink it, if a big enough area of *Titanic*'s hull was damaged.

498 The *Titanic* was wrecked on its first voyage, from Southampton, England, to New York, USA. Many rich, famous celebrities were on board. Most of them died, along with many other passengers. Only 712 of the 2232 people who sailed on *Titanic* survived.

499 **The *Titanic* crossed the Atlantic Ocean at top speed.** Late one night, off the coast of Canada, it struck a small iceberg. At first no one worried, but the hull was badly damaged and water soon gushed in. In just three hours, 'unsinkable' *Titanic* vanished beneath the waves.

▶ The *Titanic* sank in very deep water. It was rediscovered in 1985 by French and American explorers. They found out that it had broken in two before sinking. Its hull had then been crushed by water pressure, scattering debris over the ocean floor.

I. As compartments fill, the bow (front) starts to sink

2. The stern (back) of the ship begins to rise and the bow sinks more

3. The rising stern causes pressure between the third and fourth smoke stacks

4. The weak spot causes the stern of the ship to break off

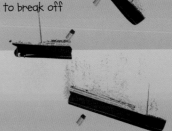

5. The stern rests in the water before sinking. The sections came to rest on the seabed some distance apart

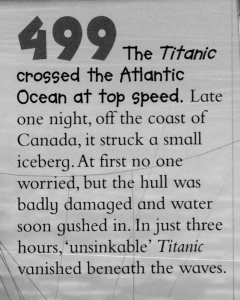

500 **Shockingly, the Titanic did not carry enough lifeboats to save every passenger.** Only 20 boats were on board. Some were launched half-empty, others were fatally overcrowded. The remaining passengers were either trapped on the Titanic and went down with it, or leapt into the water, where they drowned or died from cold.

INDEX

Page numbers in **bold** refer to main entries; page numbers in *italics* refer to illustrations.

ACKNOWLEDGEMENTS

The publishers would like to thank the following sources for the use of their photographs:
t = top, b = bottom, l = left, r = right, c = centre, bg = background, m = main

Cover: *Front* (t) Krzysztof Odziomek/Shutterstock.com, (b) Edwin van Wier/Shutterstock.com; *Spine* Cigdem Sean Cooper/Shutterstock.com; *Back* (c) David Ashley/Shutterstock.com, (r) Adisa/Shutterstock.com, (l) Tarasov/iStockphoto.com, (panel) Khoroshunova Olga/Shutterstock.com, (bl) Djmattaar/Shutterstock.com

Page 14(bg) Cathy Miles; 91(t) NASA; 131(b) Image courtesy of Monterey Bay Aquarium Research Institute c. 2007 MBARI; 176–177 National Maritime Museum, London, Greenwich Hospital Collection

Alamy 39(t) David Lyons; 40(b) Tibor Bognar; 53 WaterFrame; 195 Terry Fincher.Photo Int

Ardea 8–9 Bill Coster; 12(b) Mark Boulton; 18(t) Jean Paul Ferrero, (b) Valerie Taylor; 19 John Daniels; 20–21(b) David Dixon; 24(br) John Mason; 26 Mark Boulton; 27(b) Dae Sasitorn; 28 Jean Paul Ferrero, (br) M. Watson; 29(b) Valerie Taylor; 30(t) Mark Boulton, (b) Johan de Meester; 35(t) Jean Paul Ferrero; 42–43 Jean Paul Ferrero; 46–47 Bob Gibbons; 46(t) Thomas Dressier; 47(b) Duncan Usher; 49(t) M. Watson; 89 Kurt Amsler; 108–109 Pat Morris; 158 M.Watson

Corbis 38(b) Choo Youn-Kong/Pool/Reuters; 62(b) Frans Lanting; 84 Stephen Frink; 107 Ralph White; 159(b) Stephen Frink; 164–165 Flip Nicklin; 168(b) Images.com; 180(t) Amos Nachoum, (b) Jonathan Blair; 181 Jeffrey L. Rotman; 183 Amos Nachoum; 184 Ralph White; 186–187 Jonathan Blair; 204 Bettmann; 205 David Pollack; 206–207 Bettmann; 207; 208 Reuters; 209 epa; 210–211

Dreamstime.com 60(tl) Vintrom, (tr) Frhojdysz; 61(tr) Brento, (br) Ajalbert; 74(c) Goodolga, (b) Surub; 80(br) Johnandersonphoto; 82(t) Donsimon; 86(t) Stephankerkhofs, (b) Djmattaar; 98(t) Tommy Schultz

FLPA 37(b) D P Wilson; 39(br) ImageBroker/Imagebroker; 68(b) Mike Parry/Minden Pictures; 101(b) Fred Bavendam/Minden Pictures; 118(t) Ingo Arndt/Minden Pictures, (b) Norbert Wu/Minden Pictures; 125 Norbert Wu/Minden Pictures; 127(b) ImageBroker/Imagebroker; 151(t) Flip Nicklin/Minden Pictures; 162 Hiroya Minakuchi/Minden Pictures; 169 Tui De Roy/Minden Pictures

Fotolia 5(t) Tommy Schultz; 10(t) Deborah Benbrook; 13(tr) Michael Siller; 24 EcoView; 29(tr) Vladimir Ovchinnikov; 33(br) Vatikaki; 42(tr) Ian Scott, (l) Maribell; 49(b) Magnum; 63 Vladimir Ovchinnikov; 67(tr) khz; 71(t) Peter Schinck; 75(tl) cbpix; 98(c) Tommy Schultz; 99 Desertdiver; 100–101 cornelius; 120(t) zebra0209; 137 Alexey Khromushin

Getty Images 25(t) Brian J. Skerry; 44–45 Bloomberg via Getty Images; 45(t) Grant Duncan-Smith; 48–49 AFP/Getty Images; 85 Jeff Hunter; 106(b) Jean Tresfon; 127(t) Neil Bromhall; 132–133 Emory Kristof/National Geographic

iStockphoto.com 13(tl) shayes17; 36(tr) nealec; 41(bl) egdigital; 43(br) igs942; 59(t) Jouke van der Meer; 60(b) Dave Bluck; 61(tl) Anders Nygren; 69(bl) TSWinner; 71 Allister Clark; 81(br) Olga Khoroshunova; 98(b) tswinner; 98–99 MiguelAngeloSilva; 120(b) sethakan; 137(c) Håkan Karlsson

naturepl.com 54 Jeff Rotman; 83 Jurgen Freund; 87 Georgette Douwma; 109 Brandon Cole; 121 David Shale; 149(t) Jeff Rotman; 160(m) Mark Carwardine; 166–167 Mark Carwardine; 174 Bryan and Cherry Alexander

NOAA 96(l) W. H. F. Smith; 111(c) Archival Photography by Steve Nicklas NOS, NGS; 115 NOAA Office of Ocean Exploration, Dr. Bob Embley, NOAA PMEL; 117 Brooke et al, NOAA-OE, HBOI; 122(l) Edie Widder; 130 USS Albatross Archival Photography by Steve Nicklas, NGS, RSD, Meteor Steve Nicklas, NOS, NGS; 131 Bathysphere US Federal Government (NOAA), map W. H. F. Smith;

OceanwideImages.com 69(tr) Gary Bell; 128(c) Gary Bell; 161

photolibrary.com 52(bl) Paul Kay; 66 Paul Kay; 72 Monica & Michael Sweet; 73 Dana Edmunds; 80–81 Juniors Bildarchiv; 82(b) Wolfgang Poelzer; 90 Franco Banfi; 91(r) Reinhard Dirscherl; 123 Reinhard Dirscherl

Photoshot 54 Oceans-Image; 155(b) Woodfall

Rex features 126(c) c.W. Disney/Everett; 173 173(tr) Moviestore Collection; 179; 208–209 Newspix

Science Photo Library 45(b) Martin Bond; 50–51 Georgette Douwma; 52(tr) Planetobserver; 58 Tom McHugh; 88 Georgette Douwma; 92–93 Dr Ken Macdonald; 148–149 Christopher Swann; 173 Dolphin Inst.

SeaPics 136 Christopher Swann; 144–145

Shutterstock.com 1–2 Kristina Vackova; 5(b) Vilainecrevette; 6(b) David Ashley; 7 Andrew Jalbert; 137(b) Willyam Bradberry; 138 Shane Gross; 138(b) Shannon Workman; 141–142 Menna; 141 Jan-Dirk Hansen; 143(t) Johan_R; 143(c) Teo Dominguez; 143(b) Steve Noakes; 145 Ivan Cholakov; 146 Ami Parikh; 153 idreamphoto; 153(t) Sergey Popov V; 155(t) L.Watcharapoll; 157 Monika Wieland; 159(t) mikeledray; 160(bl) Janne Hamalainen; 161(br) Jakrit Jiraratwaro; 166 Christopher Meder; 167 Monika Wieland; 168(t) Andy.M; 172 bright; 174–175 holbox

TopFoto 175 David Fleetham; 185 2005; 204–205 Topham Picturepoint; 210; 211; 213(t) 2006, (b) Â©World History Archive

All other photographs are from: digitalSTOCK, digitalvision, Dreamstime.com, Fotolia.com, ImageState, iStockphoto.com, John Foxx, PhotoAlto, PhotoDisc, PhotoEssentials, PhotoPro, Stockbyte

All artworks from the Miles Kelly Artwork Bank

Every effort has been made to acknowledge the source and copyright holder of each picture.
Miles Kelly Publishing apologizes for any unintentional errors or omissions.